CANINE GOOD CITIZEN®

AKC Guide

Ten Essential Skills Every Well-Mannered Dog Should Know

An Official Publication of the American Kennel Club

Mary R. Burch, PhD

Canine Good Citizen, 2nd Edition

CompanionHouse Books™ is an imprint of Fox Chapel Publishing.

Project Team
Editorial Director: Kerry Bogert
Editor: Amy Deputato
Copy Editor: Colleen Dorsey
Design: Mary Ann Kahn
Index: Elizabeth Walker

ISBN 978-1-62187-191-0

Library of Congress Control Number: 2020942620

This book has been published with the intent to provide accurate and authoritative information in regard to the subject matter within. While every precaution has been taken in the preparation of this book, the author and publisher expressly disclaim any responsibility for any errors, omissions, or adverse effects arising from the use or application of the information contained herein. The techniques and suggestions are used at the reader's discretion and are not to be considered a substitute for veterinary care. If you suspect a medical problem, consult your veterinarian.

Fox Chapel Publishing
903 Square Street
Mount Joy, PA 17552

www.facebook.com/companionhousebooks

We are always looking for talented authors. To submit an idea, please send a brief inquiry to acquisitions@foxchapelpublishing.com.

Printed and bound in China
24 23 22   2 4 6 8 10 9 7 5 3

CONTENTS

ACKNOWLEDGMENTS

Canine Good Citizen: Ten Essential Skills Every Well-Mannered Dog Should Know is the definitive guide to the American Kennel Club's Canine Good Citizen (CGC) Program.

With more than 1 million dogs who have earned the CGC Award, the CGC Program is clearly the gold standard for basic training for dogs of all ages. No other dog training program has had this level of impact. This book provides how-to tips for teaching each of the ten skills, and all of the techniques suggested are based on sound behavioral principles. The Special Applications chapter presents exciting, never-before-seen information from unique CGC Programs that are considered national models. Additional information on the background of the CGC Program, the Responsible Dog Owner's Pledge, and what you can do with your dog before and after CGC makes this book relevant for every single person who owns a dog or cares about the well-being of the canines we love. Newer programs, such as the AKC Therapy Dog Program, AKC Trick Dog, and AKC FIT DOG, are also featured.

Mary R. Burch, PhD, is the Director of the AKC Family Dog Program. Dr. Burch is an award-winning dog writer and the author of twenty books, including *Volunteering with Your Pet, The Border Collie,* and *How Dogs Learn.* Dr. Burch has trained dogs to the advanced levels of obedience, and she is a Certified Applied Animal Behaviorist and a Board Certified Behavior Analyst (the human end of the leash). She is a frequent consultant on radio, on television, and in print media.

Dennis B. Sprung is the President and CEO of the American Kennel Club. He has been responsible for many other AKC books and publications, including *AKC Dog Care and Training.* Involved in the sport of dogs for more than fifty years, Mr. Sprung has been a dog owner, exhibitor, breeder, judge, AKC Delegate, and president of an all-breed club. Mr. Sprung has traveled

to dog events worldwide, and he routinely interacts with internationally recognized experts on timely dog-related topics.

David S. Woo, photographer, is a former Multimedia Specialist for the American Kennel Club, specializing in videography and photography for AKC Communications and digitization for the AKC Library and Archives. He received his BFA in Graphic Design and Video from the Maryland Institute College of Art and his MFA in Computer Arts from School of Visual Arts. Mr. Woo is one of the country's leading dog photographers, and he regularly travels to dog-related events nationwide.

We would like to recognize the following AKC staff members who reviewed information related to their subject-matter expertise:

- Carrie DeYoung
- Gina DiNardo
- Doug Ljungren
- Pam Manaton
- Heather McManus
- Caroline Murphy
- Mari-Beth O'Neill
- Daphna Straus

We would like to especially thank the hardworking, dedicated AKC Approved CGC Evaluators for the extraordinary work they do for all of the AKC Family Dog Programs.

THE NEED FOR CANINE GOOD CITIZENS

With 90 million dogs living in 68 percent of American households, dogs are more popular than ever. Currently, an astounding $70 billion are spent every year on canine toys, supplies, treats, and training books, attesting to the fact that dog owners love their dogs and want what's best for them. But despite a proliferation of information about dogs in printed and digital media, there are some problems with dog ownership in the United States. Why?

More and more people have taken on the responsibility of dog ownership, but, lacking time and understanding about their dog's needs, some dog owners are not raising well-behaved canine companions. Problems ranging from nuisance barking to attacks against children have many communities responding with restrictive laws and deep concern. "No Dogs Allowed" signs abound in privately owned businesses and residential areas. People with poorly trained dogs, those they come in contact with, and the dogs themselves are suffering.

The American Kennel Club® (AKC ®) Canine Good Citizen® (CGC ®) Program is the answer to the pressing question of how to ensure that all dogs are well-behaved, welcome members of any community. Not just another training guide, this is the first and only book to provide a prescriptive approach and a detailed curriculum based on sound behavioral principles for obtaining the Canine Good Citizen award from the AKC.

The AKC, the nation's leading authority on dogs in the United States for more than 135 years, developed the CGC Program as the gold standard of training for every dog in America, regardless of age or breed. All dogs—purebreds and mixed breeds alike—are welcome in the CGC Program. Whether you decide to earn the CGC certificate or not, this book will provide you with the foundation you need to be a responsible dog owner, and it will show you how to teach your dog the skills he needs to be a well-mannered pet.

Never before has there been such a critical need for the AKC Canine Good Citizen Program or for a simple-to-use, informative book that prepares dogs to earn the Canine Good Citizen award. In the 1950s, families across America sat in front of their black-and-white televisions to watch *Lassie*, the nation's image of the ideal dog. This wonderful, beautiful Collie would instantly come when called, jump through a window on command, and instinctively find the little boy who was lost. Viewers were impressed with the concept of a well-trained dog, and during these *Leave It to Beaver* years, dogs came to be thought of as family members.

However, by the 1980s, problems caused by irresponsible dog owners had dramatically changed and damaged the reputation of man's best friend. As a result

Fiona, a Bernese Mountain Dog, was the one-millionth dog to pass the AKC's Canine Good Citizen Test. AKC President Dennis Sprung awards a commemorative plaque to Fiona and her proud owner, Nora Pavone.

of the graphic media coverage of several maulings and deaths caused by dogs, 1980s America found itself in the midst of what the press described as "pit bull hysteria." The coverage of pit bull attacks lent an unnecessary stigma to all larger, muscular dogs. Many emotionally charged articles and televised reports neglected to mention that these horrible incidents were not the dogs' fault, and that any bad feelings should be targeted at the dogs' owners. In the 1980s, an increasing number of state and local governments passed legislation that placed restrictions on dog ownership.

Since the year 2000, these restrictions have continued to increase in a growing number of municipalities. For example, in some places, there are limits on the number of dogs per household as well as all-out bans on dogs in certain housing and recreational

The American Kennel Club's Canine Good Citizen Test is an evaluation of the basic skills that every dog should know. The ten test items are:

1. Accepting a Friendly Stranger
2. Sitting Politely for Petting
3. Appearance and Grooming
4. Out for a Walk
5. Walking through a Crowd
6. Sit and Down on Command/Staying in Place
7. Coming When Called
8. Reaction to Another Dog
9. Reaction to Distractions
10. Supervised Separation

areas. Specific breeds have been outlawed from entire cities and counties, and, as a result, families have been forced to find other homes for their pets, sometimes being given only days to do so.

To offset restrictive legislation and dog-related problems, the American Kennel Club's Canine Good Citizen Program is doing its part to teach dog owners to be responsible. In 2019, Fiona, a Bernese Mountain Dog owned by Nora Pavone of Brooklyn, New York, became the one-millionth dog to earn the CGC title. As more dog owners embrace the CGC Responsible Dog Owner's Pledge and provide their dogs with CGC training, we can turn communities everywhere into places where dogs are welcomed.

Long aware of the need to protect the rights of people who love their dogs, the AKC implemented the CGC Program in 1989 with the goal of promoting responsible dog ownership and recognizing dogs for good behavior both at home and in the community. Several versions of the evaluation were field-tested with hundreds of dogs before the program was implemented at the national level. In its current format, the CGC Award shows a commitment to responsible dog ownership, and passing the ten-item CGC Test means that a dog is under basic instructional control, can respond to simple verbal cues while on leash, and, most important, is reliable in the presence of people and other animals.

These are the skills that should be part of every dog's basic education. In addition to having owners teach their dogs basic good manners, the comprehensive CGC Program also educates owners about the responsibilities of ownership so that they can enjoy their dogs to the fullest.

The CGC Program is a noncompetitive program open to all dogs, purebreds and mixed breeds alike. The heart of the CGC Program is the CGC Test, which assesses the ability of a dog to be a well-behaved member of the community. The CGC certificate or title that is earned by passing the test proves the owner's commitment to having a well-mannered dog.

There are an increasing number of benefits for those who have earned the CGC award. For example, in some locations, CGC dogs gain access to dog parks and hiking trails, and certain apartment buildings and condominiums require that dogs have their CGC certificates before their owners are permitted to move in with them. Several of this country's largest service and therapy dog organizations require dogs to pass the CGC Test as a prerequisite for therapy dog work. In addition to therapy dog work, CGC provides the perfect foundation for many other AKC programs, including AKC FIT DOG, AKC Trick Dog, agility, obedience, Rally, and more.

Many 4-H groups have added CGC as the curriculum for beginning dog training. And as of 2019, 48 states and the United States Senate have passed Canine Good Citizen resolutions, showing that our nation's legislators support the CGC Program as a means of increasing responsible dog ownership and ensuring that well-mannered dogs remain welcome in our communities.

This book will help you teach your dog the skills for each of the ten CGC Test Items. You'll learn the exercises, how to teach them, how to practice at home, and special considerations for teaching each skill. Scenarios are given to illustrate the importance of each of the CGC Test Items, and behavioral concepts are explained so that you

understand the reasoning behind the recommendations.

There are many training philosophies and effective methods for training dogs. In this book, we describe an approach based on positive reinforcement. In the Finding CGC Training and Testing Near You chapter on page 140, you'll learn how to find the trainer who best meets the needs of you and your dog. The sections at the beginning of each chapter explain the actual test items as described in the Canine Good Citizen Evaluator Guide.

The Canine Good Citizen title proves an owner's commitment to training.

ACCEPTING A FRIENDLY STRANGER

This test demonstrates that the dog will allow a friendly stranger to approach him and speak to the handler in a natural, everyday situation.

The test begins with the dog seated at the handler's side. The Evaluator walks up to the dog and handler and greets the handler in a friendly manner, ignoring the dog. The Evaluator and handler exchange pleasantries (e.g., "Hello, it's good to see you again"). In this test, the Evaluator does not interact with the dog. The Evaluator and handler stand close enough to do a pretend handshake.

- The dog must show no sign of resentment, aggression, or shyness.
- The dog may not jump on or rush to the Evaluator to initiate contact. The dog may not lunge forward to greet the Evaluator.
- The dog should be under control throughout the exercise. If the handler must use excessive corrections (e.g., trying to hold the dog to prevent jumping) to control the dog, the dog should not pass the exercise.

We've all met them when we're out in public—those happy, friendly, exuberant dogs who jump on us to say hello. We approach to greet the owner of such a dog, and, within seconds, we're being pounced on and receiving a heartfelt, slurpy, wet kiss from a spirited, furry bundle of joy. For those of us who love dogs, there are times when delightful canine kisses are welcome and we're happy to receive them. But sometimes, such as when we're enjoying a quiet walk or wearing business clothes, being jumped on by a frisky dog without an invitation may not be a good thing.

But never mind the business clothes. Some people are flat-out afraid of dogs. When an overzealous 60-pound canine-greeting-committee-of-one lunges and appears to be out of control, these individuals find themselves feeling fearful and uncomfortable even though the dog is offering a well-intended, convivial greeting. Dogs who give greetings that are so enthusiastic that a person can be knocked down or scratched are not suitable as canine "therapists" in nursing homes and other therapy settings until they receive further training.

Is it ever acceptable for a dog to jump up on a person to say hello, jump into someone's lap, or rush up to someone in excitement? It might be, but the key here

Since changes related to COVID-19 in 2020, the "handshake" in CGC is a pretend handshake or a head nod.

is whether the dog has been invited to initiate physical contact with the "friendly stranger." Remember that being a responsible dog owner means that your dog never infringes on the rights of another person. Even a friendly dog should not jump up on a person you meet on the street or into someone's lap without an invitation.

When you and your dog meet someone in public, being overly excited to see the person is not the only problematic thing that a dog can do. Some dogs are at the opposite end of affability. These are the extremely shy dogs that may hide behind their owners when a stranger approaches, pull away from an unfamiliar person, or, in some cases, urinate inappropriately.

Meeting a friendly stranger in a calm, collected manner is a skill that every dog needs in order to be well regarded by people other than his owner. Meeting new people falls into the category of socialization. Socialization means learning to interact with others in a manner that is acceptable. Dogs need to be socialized to deal with people outside of their families as well as with other dogs. Socializing your dog is one of the most important things you can do as a responsible owner. Socialization activities can begin when the dog is a puppy and should continue throughout his life.

The "friendly stranger" in the CGC Test is someone who simulates a person you might meet when you and your dog are out for a walk. In this test item, when the Evaluator

In CGC Test Item 1, Accepting a Friendly Stranger, the Evaluator interacts with the handler. Interacting with the dog comes in later exercises. The handshake is pictured to show the distance at which the Evaluator meets the dog and handler; there is no longer a handshake in the CGC Test.

approaches, you will say hello, do a pretend handshake or elbow bump, and have a brief interaction. The friendly stranger in a CGC Test is a person who does not live in the dog's household, is not an instructor who has been handling the dog every week in class, and is not a canine professional or a relative who knows the dog very well.

In this segment of the test, the point of the exercise is for the dog to behave acceptably when his owner meets and interacts briefly with a stranger. The stranger does not talk to or pet the dog; this will happen in subsequent exercises.

Why Socialization Is Important

Adequate socialization is the key to owning a dog that is happy, well adjusted, and eager to meet new people. Dogs that are well socialized are friendly and biddable (easily managed). They create the impression to others that they are safe animals with reliable, predictable behavior. Dogs that are good citizens demonstrate impeccable canine manners. These are dogs that accept friendly strangers and are welcome members of the community.

In addition to being well mannered and well liked, there is another important reason for every dog to have CGC skills. These days, dog owners in general are losing their rights because some owners are not responsible. Breed-specific legislation (BSL) has been proposed or passed in a number of states. BSL

DID YOU KNOW?

Small dogs benefit from Canine Good Citizen training. Without socialization, small dogs can develop a fear of new people and situations.

is legislation that targets certain breeds. When a law is proposed that says no more dogs of a specific breed can live in a particular city, this is an example of BSL. BSL targets a breed as a whole, with no regard for the good behavior or advanced training of individual dogs within the breed. This type of legislation restricts the rights of dog owners and, in most cases, targets specific medium to large breeds. Because many people perceive that large dogs are dangerous, it is critical that dog owners teach their dogs to meet people in a controlled manner. It is the *deed* that matters, not the *breed*.

Small dogs also need socialization. Socializing small dogs teaches them useful skills, such as how to walk on leash and how to interact with people and other animals. The adequate socialization of toy breeds results in dogs that are confident and unafraid of the world around them.

Understanding Socialization

Socialization means interacting with (or socializing with) others. Socialization is also a broader concept that involves exposing dogs to people, places, situations, sounds, other dogs, and other species that may be in the dog's life, such as cats, birds, or horses. Properly socializing your dog means providing continuing exposure to the world so that your dog becomes self-assured and unafraid of new experiences.

In a newborn litter, the very first socialization a puppy will receive will be from his dam (mother) and littermates. As a matter of fact, there is actually a period of time when the puppy is still with his litter that is referred to as the *socialization period*.

A well-socialized dog is happy to meet new friends and will behave calmly while doing so.

These AKC S.T.A.R. Puppy graduates are off to a great start for future success in the CGC Program.

In the first two weeks of life, puppies spend about 90 percent of their time sleeping. In these early days, before they even open their eyes, sweet little neonatal puppies will turn to Mom and littermates to keep warm. In a normal litter, the third week of life is marked by the puppies' opening their eyes, tottering around on legs that are unsteady, and beginning to interact with their littermates by chewing on their ears and crawling over them.

When the puppies are three to twelve weeks old, the socialization period is taking place. This is when puppies begin to develop social relationships with the people and other dogs (their dam and littermates) in their lives. When puppies have no exposure to human contact during the socialization period, it will be difficult for them to adjust to people as they get older. They become dogs that may have a difficult time bonding with humans and may be difficult to train. It is absolutely possible to train dogs that had a bad start in life, but there may be some additional challenges along the way.

Similarly, if puppies are for some reason separated from the litter at a very young age, it may be hard for them when they get older to develop appropriate relationships with other dogs. These puppies may grow up to be either extremely fearful of other dogs or pushy and dominant because they've never been taught to relate to members of their own species.

One of the most important lessons a puppy learns from his dam and siblings is *bite inhibition*. Bite inhibition is when a dog intentionally controls the intensity of a bite. In the litter, when a puppy is nursing, if he bites the dam too hard, she will nip him or stand up and walk away, teaching a valuable lesson by leaving—and taking breakfast with her. The puppy soon learns that he needs to control himself and that biting hard is not OK.

When puppies in a litter are playing their rough-and-tumble games, sometimes a puppy will get carried away and bite a sibling just a little too hard. The sibling might jump up and yelp. He may leave the game or may growl, snap, or bark as if to say, "Don't do that! That hurts!" The puppy learns that if he wants the fun game with his littermate to continue, he cannot bite too hard.

Responsible breeders start providing socialization activities for puppies as young as two weeks old. Breeders will hold and massage puppies and provide other gentle stimulation, such as playing music and introducing new sounds. As the pups get a little older, friends are invited to visit and hold the puppies so that, from the time they are very young, the puppies are accustomed to meeting people. By the time a puppy comes to your home, a responsible breeder will have taken that puppy for rides in the car and on trips to the veterinarian's office. The puppy will have been exposed to a crate, and a house-training schedule will have been implemented.

Socialization at Home

So you've adopted a puppy or an older dog, and you've brought him home. Now what? If you got a rescue dog, a dog from a shelter, or a dog that had a rough start in life, your dog needs socialization at home and in the community. Even if he came from a responsible breeder who did everything right until the day you took the dog home, your dog still needs socialization at home and in the community. Socialization is not something that should be addressed for a short time and then stopped. If you are a responsible owner, socializing your dog will be an ongoing activity that occurs as a natural part of everyday living.

To make sure that your dog continues to have good relationships with people and other animals, the first step you should take is to build a bond with your new companion through play and activities. Daily puppy playtime for dogs of all ages has tremendous value. In puppy playtime, you continue the activities of the litter. Structured daily play will be an activity that your dog will look forward to throughout his life.

A Well-Socialized Dog

Some dogs are mellow. Their behavior and temperament are such that from the time they were puppies, they were calm when meeting new people. Some owners who attend CGC classes are lucky in that, on the very first night, before any instruction at all, their dogs can naturally pass the Accepting a Friendly Stranger CGC Test Item. If you happen to be an owner with an extremely mellow dog that meets new people in a

cool, collected way, you can focus on teaching other new skills. Remember, though, that socialization should be an ongoing part of every dog's education, and your courteous canine will always benefit from a chance to meet new people.

When dogs have a problem with meeting new people, it usually involves one of two situations: either the dog is overly exuberant or the dog is extremely shy. Both of these problems can be addressed with training and exposure to new people. Before starting CGC training, you can check to see if your dog needs training to accept a stranger. Take your dog (or puppy) for a walk in your

A socialized dog is a polite companion out in public.

neighborhood or at a local park. When someone approaches, allow the person to come over and pet the dog.

What does your dog do when an unfamiliar person approaches and speaks to you? If your dog stands calmly and is under control while being petted, you're one step ahead of the game. Does the dog try to jump on the stranger, pull away, hide behind you, or lunge at the stranger in excitement? If you see any of these behaviors, you'll need to do some training. Accepting a friendly stranger will allow your dog and you to confidently meet anyone in public and have a pleasant and enjoyable experience.

Different Personalities
Exuberant Dogs

The exuberant dog is one that has a very high activity level. This is the extremely energetic, high-spirited dog. This type of buoyant, effervescent dog is a joy to own after he has learned some manners. Before learning CGC manners, he may bounce and spin, pulling his owner toward any unfamiliar person who is approaching. Exuberant dogs can be easily overstimulated; however, one trick to working with these dogs is to very systematically expose them to new people, situations, and other animals.

For the CGC Test, you're going to teach your dog to sit (see Test Item 2) while the "friendly stranger" approaches. For dogs that need work on socialization, in addition to teaching skills such as sit at home or in a class, you'll want to take your dog on regular "field trips" in the community. These outings will give you and your dog plenty of opportunities to meet new people.

Shy Dogs

When it comes to accepting a friendly stranger, shy dogs may need some training and experience in order to pass this CGC Test Item. As with dogs that are exuberant, shaping behaviors slowly works well with shy dogs. Shy dogs can be gradually desensitized to new people who approach and greet their owners. When working with a dog that is shy or fearful, it is important that you don't give the dog a lot of attention for being shy. While some reassurance to build confidence is OK, if you coddle and give a great deal of attention to the trembling dog each time an unfamiliar person approaches to say hello, you'll soon have a dog that is fearful with everyone. A better response than coddling a shy dog is to teach your dog to meet new people in a confident manner. The shy dog can benefit from behavioral exercises designed to teach the dog that good things come from meeting new people.

Small Dogs

There's an unfortunate trend for some dog owners to carry toy breeds everywhere they go. Some might even dress their dogs in clothes that match their own outfits. Toy breeds (along with other small breeds and small mixed-breed dogs) aren't fashion accessories. Toy breeds aren't babies. Toy breeds don't benefit from lives in which their feet are never permitted to touch the ground. All dogs, including those who are pint-sized, deserve to have the training and socialization provided by the CGC Program.

If you meet or see a toy-breed dog that appears to quiver and shake when a new person approaches, chances are you're looking at a dog that has not been trained or adequately socialized. Signs of distress in a small dog will include a submissive lifting of the paw, trembling, or attempting to pull away from the person who is greeting his owner. If you've ever seen this happen, and this is your impression of small dogs, don't let them fool you.

Toy breeds may be small in size, but when well trained and properly socialized, they are confident dogs with huge personalities. All you have to do is attend AKC events to see well-socialized small dogs in action, succeeding at obedience, excelling in agility, and doing a great job in the fun sport of Rally. Every weekend, in CGC Tests

Despite their portable size, small dogs are not accessories. They need to be socialized and trained like any other dog.

across the country, small dogs pass fair and square, holding their own among the larger breeds that are typically known to do well in training activities.

And don't forget the wonderful socialization opportunities provided to small dogs that participate in conformation. Conformation shows are bustling, crowded events. While toy breeds entered in conformation may be carried by their handlers to the ring to keep their coats clean for showing, these are dogs that will confidently strut on a leash (just watch them in the ring) in the very distracting setting of a dog show. They accept many friendly strangers in the form of judges.

What about small dogs that come from shelters or rescues? Small dogs and puppies are the most likely dogs to be adopted. Shelters and rescue groups may be particularly selective about toy-breed and small-dog adoptions, choosing homes that will provide training and socialization opportunities for these remarkable little dogs.

Using Desensitization to Teach New Behaviors

The behavioral procedure in which you systematically expose a dog to new situations is called *desensitization*. Desensitization involves using a hierarchy that ranges from the least to the most problematic situations. For example, if your dog is afraid of wheelchairs, you could bring him into a room in which a wheelchair is sitting in the corner. Eventually, you could move the dog closer to the wheelchair. Then, you could have the dog walk close to the unmoving wheelchair and, finally, have the chair wheeled toward your dog.

Desensitization can be used to teach shy dogs to accept new people and objects.

To use desensitization to teach acceptance of a friendly stranger, you can manipulate several of the behavior's components (including the distance your dog is from the new person, meeting a familiar versus an unfamiliar person, the length of time a person interacts with you, and meeting a person who is low-key versus one who is very animated). In all CGC exercises and training, the dog is on a leash.

The Accepting a Friendly Stranger exercise lays the foundation for a dog's good manners when in social situations.

Above and Beyond Accepting a Friendly Stranger

When your dog can perform all of the exercises mentioned on page 8 (meaning that he sits calmly while you are greeted by an unfamiliar person), you can practice exercises that are more difficult. CGC Test Items 2, 3, 4, 5, 8, and 9 expand on the Accepting a Friendly Stranger exercise by having the dog tolerate petting and handling, walking on a leash and through a crowd of people, and reacting appropriately in the presence of other dogs and distractions. Once your dog has mastered Accepting a Friendly Stranger, you're on your way to earning the CGC award.

Training Your Dog to Accept a Friendly Stranger

1. Take your dog for a walk in a local park, at a pet-supply store, or somewhere else where you will encounter other people. Have your dog sit at your left side as a person walks by, about 15 feet (4.5m) away. Can your dog do this without becoming overly excited?
2. If the dog will sit at your side while someone passes 15 feet (4.5m) away from you, have the dog sit at your side while someone passes 10 feet (3m) away. If the dog is excitable and jumps out of the sit position or attempts to pull you toward the person, increase the distance. You can also practice sitting by giving your dog reminders, such as "Sit...sit, good dog," and rewarding with food if you are using food rewards.

3. When the dog will sit at your side as someone passes 10 feet (3m) away, you're ready to repeat these steps with someone 5 feet (1.5m) away.

4. When your dog will sit and watch a person pass at a distance of 5 feet (1.5m) away, do the exercise again. This time, speak to the person, saying something brief, such as "Nice day, isn't it?" Watch how your dog responds. If he behaves acceptably when you speak to someone who is 5 feet (1.5m) away, you're ready for the next step.

5. At this point, you may need a helper. You can ask a friend, neighbor, or someone in your training class to help you with this. Instruct the helper to stand about 15 feet (4.5m) away from you and your dog and wait for you to signal that he or she should approach. With your dog at your left side, get the dog to sit and then give the signal for your helper to approach. The helper should say something like "Hi, how are you?" You answer, and the helper walks away. In this exercise, the helper does not speak to or touch the dog.

If the dog tries to jump on the person, you should prompt the dog to sit, and then reward the sitting behavior. For some dogs, this exercise could require several days of practice in which the helper begins at 15 feet (4.5m) away and then stops at 5 feet (1.5m) away to verbally greet you and your dog. If a shy dog tries to hide behind you during this exercise, do not pick the dog up and hold him in your arms.

6. Continue to practice the exercise in Step 5. Vary the helpers who approach to greet you. Make sure that your dog experiences an adult male, an adult female, and a child greeting you.

7. In addition to varying the people who will approach and act as friendly strangers (i.e., male, female, younger, older), you should have your helpers vary the style in which they interact with you. Initially, a helper can greet

In the Accepting a Friendly Stranger exercise, the dog will begin the exercise by sitting as the "stranger" approaches.

you with very flat affect. A bored-sounding, quiet voice will not frighten a dog that is wary of strangers. As your dog successfully meets people and shows the ability to be calm and unafraid, you can have the helper approach with greetings that are increasingly animated. An excited-sounding friendly stranger can rush up and say in a louder voice, "Hey, how ya doing?" The ability to respond to all types of behavior is required for a dog that is steady in the community. This skill is also a requirement for therapy dogs, who may encounter people speaking loudly or moving quickly in therapy settings.

8. As your dog becomes steady when an unfamiliar person approaches and briefly exchanges pleasantries with you (e.g., "Hi, how are you? Nice to see you."), extend the length of time from a brief verbal exchange to a conversation.

9. Remember that socialization means exposure to new things as well as to new people. When you're on walks or outings, give your dog a chance to walk on different surfaces, such as grass, concrete, and slick floors. Encourage your dog to jump over low obstacles on a trail and to walk with you on a sidewalk (on leash, of course) near busy traffic.

10. In the preceding exercises, you can have the stranger give your dog a treat. This will help your dog learn that good things come from interacting nicely with other people.

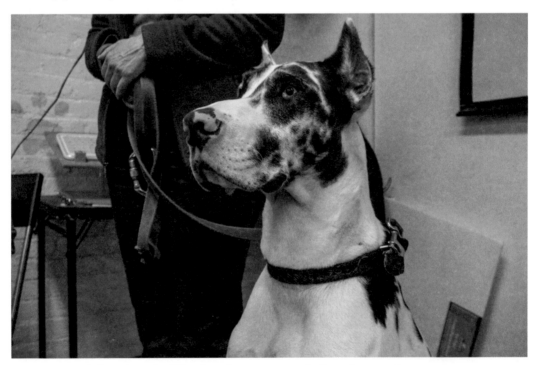

No dogs—especially large dogs—should be allowed to jump on people. Sitting by your side encourages polite behavior.

PREPARING FOR CGC

You can begin training in the comfort of your own living room or backyard, but a dog with CGC skills is one that is well socialized and has the manners for community living, so you'll eventually want to do some training in public settings. You can "graduate" from the living room to the street in front of your house, then to walking around the block, then to going to a nearby park, and eventually to training in active areas such as a dog club, a public park, or a pet-supply store.

Using this book, you can prepare for the CGC Test on your own, but attending a CGC or basic training class is always an excellent idea. In classes with other dogs and people, you have access to assistance and additional training tips as well as to helpers (who can be your friendly strangers) and distraction dogs. In cases where you have a dog that is afraid of men or children, attending a class will provide your dog with opportunities to interact with them. If you decide to attend a training class, ideally you should find one designed specifically for teaching CGC skills. However, if such a class is not available in your area, a basic obedience training class can teach many of the elements of CGC. Be sure to tell the instructor of a basic class that passing the CGC Test is your goal.

SITTING POLITELY FOR PETTING

This test demonstrates that the dog will allow a friendly stranger to touch him while he is out with his handler.

With the dog sitting at the handler's side (either side is permissible) to begin the test, the Evaluator approaches and asks, "May I pet your dog?" The Evaluator then pets the dog on the head and body. The handler may talk to his or her dog throughout the exercise. After petting the dog, the Evaluator may circle the dog or simply back away to begin the next test item.

- The dog must show no signs of shyness or resentment.
- As the Evaluator begins to pet the dog, the dog may stand to receive petting.
- The dog may not struggle and pull away to avoid petting.
- The dog may move slightly forward to receive petting but should not lunge at the Evaluator or rush or jump forward.
- The dog may appear to be happy about the contact with the Evaluator and may have some body movements.
- The dog should appear to be under control throughout the exercise.

It's a crisp, clear fall day, and there's no better way to celebrate one of nature's most perfect gifts than taking your dog to a local park for a peaceful, long walk on the trails. Off you go, just you and your new dog. The exhilaration that comes from an experience like this is the reason that many people decide to add four-legged friends to their families. You're relishing the cool breeze, and your dog is having great fun on his end of the leash, sniffing the trail and enjoying the scenery. Within minutes, people begin passing you on the trail.

With the CGC award as a goal, you've been working on teaching your dog how to accept friendly strangers (CGC Test Item 1), so when strangers pass and say hello, your dog behaves beautifully. Sooner or later, though, you're going to learn a secret about dogs. The secret is that dogs and puppies are proven people magnets, and the dog lovers in this world are plentiful. When dog lovers see a dog, they want to touch, hug, ask questions about, and interact with this wonderful canine creature.

For the dog that is just beginning CGC training, strangers passing by, saying hello, and commenting on the gorgeous weather is one thing. However, having an enthusiastic person pause to pet, embrace, and make a fuss over your dog is another story. With some untrained dogs (as well as those who are just beginning training), once the petting from a stranger begins, they turn into wiggling, spinning, jumping, giddy bundles of silliness. Some dogs may roll over when they are petted, and a very active dog may jump on the

So that dogs remain well-respected members of our communities, every dog should be calm and non-threatening when meeting people.

unsuspecting person. These behaviors can be signs of an enthusiastic or excited dog; the dog that rolls over to expose his belly may be submissive or shy. Training is needed to correct any of these less-than-perfect greeting behaviors, and Item 2 (Sitting Politely for Petting) of the CGC Test is precisely where this training is evaluated.

Many dogs lose control when they are introduced to humans they've never met; these dogs need CGC training. In contrast, after some wiggling and wagging of happy tails, some canines have the impressive ability to use their most impeccable manners when greeting people for the first time. They'll sit quietly and tolerate petting, making the humans who meet them feel comfortable and appreciated. In animal-assisted therapy settings, these are the well-respected dogs that are considered to be reliable and safe.

Perhaps because of a lack of experience around people or limited exposure to humans early in life, some dogs may not respond well to petting. Such a dog might look away, appearing aloof and disinterested in the eager person who is trying his hardest to make a new canine friend. The not-so-social, disinterested dog may actually move away from a person who attempts to pet him.

If you have a dog or puppy like this, don't despair. Daily playtime with you, paired with training and socialization, can be effective components of a program designed to teach your dog to be more socially oriented. When your dog can consistently perform CGC Test Item 2, you'll have a dog that can meet new people in public and will greet visitors to your home in a way that makes every guest feel welcomed—by you and your dog.

Teaching Dogs to Sit Politely for Petting

With practice and frequent exposure, the dog has already learned CGC Test Item 1: Accepting a Friendly Stranger. This exercise required the dog to stay composed and collected while an unfamiliar person approached and talked to you, the dog's owner.

In this next exercise, your canine companion will learn to sit at your side while an unfamiliar person approaches, speaks to you, reaches out, and pets him. By having an unfamiliar person pet your dog while the dog remains under control, we're upping the ante and getting to the heart of what Canine Good Citizen training is all about. CGC dogs make people feel comfortable.

Sitting politely for petting is a skill that consists of three primary components for the dog: (1) sitting on cue, (2) tolerating petting, and (3) sitting while being petted by someone other than the owner. For the skills on the CGC Test, we provide you with methods and training tips. Remember that an experienced instructor can help you choose the training methods that can work best for you and your dog.

The first step in the Sitting Politely for Petting exercise is to get your dog into the sitting position.

When the dog is sitting, the Evaluator will approach and pet the dog.

Why Is "Sit" So Important?

Teaching your dog to sit on command, or cue, is one of the easiest things to teach, yet it is one of the most important skills your dog will ever learn. There may be a time when you teach your dog an advanced skill, such as weaving through poles on an agility course, that is completely new to the dog and something that dogs do not do naturally. However, your dog already knows how to sit. Your job will be to teach the dog to sit on cue.

In behavioral terms, we say that you are gaining *stimulus control* with regard to the dog's sitting. A behavior is said to be under stimulus control when it occurs as a result of a stimulus that is presented. So, if you say "Sit," and the dog sits, sitting is under stimulus control with regard to your verbal instructions. If you have to say "Sit" four times and physically assist the dog to sit, the verbal cue for sit is not under good stimulus control.

Sitting on cue is one of the most critical building blocks for training any dog; a reliable sit is a part of the foundation upon which the rest of your dog's training will be built. In the extreme sense, being able to sit on cue is a skill that could save your dog's life. If, for some reason, your dog was off leash across the street and a car was coming, calling the dog to you would be a bad choice. However, knowing that the dog will sit on cue, you could say "Jake, sit!" in a loud voice to get the dog into a safe, stationary position.

When a dog is sitting politely at his owner's side, other people feel comfortable around him. Shy dogs, who first learn to tolerate petting, can eventually learn to enjoy it.

No matter the situation, sitting is a basic behavior for good manners. This dog is being evaluated in an AKC Temperament Test.

There are two primary uses for the sit. The first is as a skill that can be used in your daily routine and in activities you do with your dog. For example, if someone comes to visit, you can instruct your dog to sit while greeting the visitor. At times when your hands are full or you need the dog to be still, you can instruct a trained dog to sit. Here's an example of using the sit command in this fashion: you're taking your dog on a therapy visit, and when you get out of your car, you need to gather your computer case, your purse, and some supplies. You could get the dog out first and put him in a sit-stay (we'll be learning the stay later on) while you collect your supplies.

In AKC obedience and Rally competition, dogs are required to do automatic sits as part of heeling patterns. In agility, the fast-moving sport in which dogs complete an obstacle course, many handlers choose to leave their dogs in a sit at the start line. There is also an obstacle called the "pause table" in agility on which the judge sometimes asks the handler to make the dog sit.

The second use for the sit on cue is to use it as a behavior control technique. As mentioned previously, if a dog is extremely excitable around new people, you can teach your dog to sit while greeting people to prevent him from jumping up. This strategy uses the behavioral technique called DRI, or differential reinforcement of incompatible behavior. DRI means that you will select a behavior to reward (in this case, the sit) that is incompatible with the behavior you are trying to eliminate (jumping up on people).

Teaching Your Dog to Sit on Cue

In CGC Test Item 2 (Sitting Politely for Petting), you are going to string together three behaviors: sitting on command, tolerating petting, and sitting while being petted by someone other than you. Two methods for teaching the sit on command are provided here.

The first method involves using food to guide the dog to sit. When food is used to guide the dog into position, trainers sometimes refer to this as using food as a lure. Using food to guide the dog means that the trainer moves the food around, and the dog moves into position in order to get to the food. This is different from using food as a reinforcer or reward, which means that the dog gets the food after performing the behavior in order to increase the likelihood that he will continue doing the desired behavior.

The second method of teaching the sit on command involves giving the dog physical guidance (or physical prompts) to get him into position. Physical guidance means that the trainer actually touches the dog and very gently moves him into the correct position.

Method 1: Using Food

1. Get yourself ready. Choose a time when you have about twenty uninterrupted minutes that you can devote to a training session. Your dog will be on a leash and collar. You've already selected your food (or toy) reinforcers based on the reinforcer sampling (see sidebar) you did before starting training. If food is your reinforcer, get your treat bag or put a few pieces of food in your pocket.

   In some cases, dogs are more motivated by toys than they are by food. If this is the case for your dog, you can use a toy to guide the dog into position in the following exercises. Where we suggest you reward the dog with food, you'll give the dog the toy or ball to hold for a few seconds.

   We suggest that at the beginning of each training session, you cheerfully say something to your dog to let him know that this is time for training. You can say something like "Let's work!" to let the dog know what is happening. Your dog will soon learn to recognize training time. Be sure to bring along a ball, a toy, or something else that your dog has fun with. When "work" is over, reward him with play and fun with you.

2. Stand in front of the dog. Your toes will be about 1 foot (30.5cm) away from the dog's front paws, and the dog will be standing. Hold a piece of food in your hand as you stand in front of the dog. Let the dog see the food.

3. Move the food so you are holding it slightly (about 2 to 4 inches [5 to 10cm]) higher than the dog's head and in front of his eyes (about 6 inches [15cm] away).

REINFORCER SAMPLING

Reinforcer sampling is the process in which a trainer allows a dog to come into contact with potential reinforcers (rewards) to determine which reinforcers are likely to be most effective in training. Basically, reinforcer sampling involves trying a variety of treats, toys, and other positive consequences to find out what the dog likes best.

4. Now, holding the food, move your hand (now slightly higher than the dog's head) toward the back of the dog's head. Your hand should be moving parallel to the floor. This motion will cause the dog to look up so that he can visually follow the food. Looking up and tipping his head back will cause the dog to rock back into the sit position without your touching him.

    Remember, when you hold the food above the dog's head, it should be only about 2 to 4 inches (5 to 10cm) above the dog. If you hold the food too high, there is a good chance that you'll accidentally teach your dog to jump for the food. If you hold the food too low, the dog is likely to simply reach out and take the food without sitting.

5. Give the verbal cue "Sit" in a calm, unemotional, flat but firm, normal voice. Avoid "up-speech" when you give your dog a cue. Up-speech is when statements are expressed as questions, as in "Sit?" This indicates to the dog that you are not in charge and are not sure of yourself.

6. The timing of when you say "Sit" is extremely important. If you say "Sit" before the dog knows what is happening and before you are in position, he will ignore you, and then you will have taught your dog that he can ignore you and your instructions. Say "Sit" just as you move the food back over the dog's head, his back legs start to bend, and he is moving into the sit position.

7. As soon as the dog is in a sit position (rear end on the floor), say "Good boy!" (or whatever verbal praise you choose to use). Give the dog the food reward at the same time as you're saying "Good boy!" Thus, as soon as he sits, you praise him and give him the food.

8. Initially, your dog can sit momentarily (for a second or two) and then, after praising and giving the reward, you can say "OK!" (or whatever word you want to use to release the dog) and take a step away to have the dog stand up.

9. As your dog becomes more proficient with sitting on command, things will happen faster, and you'll be able to eliminate some of these steps. You will be able to stand in front of the dog, holding the food as in Step 3, and the dog will quickly sit when you say "Sit." When this happens, give the dog the food and praise; you won't need to do Step 4.

10. As a final step in teaching the sit on cue with you standing in front of the dog, hold the food in your hand at your side as you say "Sit," and the dog will sit without being guided by the food. Reward and praise the dog.

As your puppy learns the sit, he will get used to your hand motions, so you can phase out the food.

- Stand with your dog beside you (on leash). Have the dog sit on cue at your side. When a dog competes in obedience events, he is required to sit and heel on the handler's left side. In the CGC Test, a dog may sit on either side—this is the handler's choice. Requiring that dogs work on the left side in formal obedience is a decades-old tradition that originally came from hunting. Most people are right-handed and would carry their rifles with their right hands; therefore, they would work their dogs on the left side. In competition events, the left side is used so that every competitor experiences the same heeling patterns and exercises. We suggest that if you plan on doing any other training activities with your dog, teach the dog heel and sit on your left side to avoid confusion later on.

- Start walking with your dog, stop, and instruct the dog to sit. You can revert to using food to guide the dog if needed, but phase out the food as soon as possible.

- In your house or another location where the dog is 100 percent reliable when off leash, practice having the dog sit on cue when you are several feet (about a meter) away.

- After your dog sits with no help from you, begin extending the length of time that you require him to sit (e.g., five seconds, then ten, twenty, thirty, etc.). For formal obedience, to earn the first title (Novice A), a dog is required to sit for one minute while his handler stands on the other side of the ring.

Method 2: Using Physical Prompting

Physical prompting is when a trainer puts his hands on the dog and guides the dog into position. For example, in using physical prompting to teach a dog to stand with his front paws on the edge of a bed, the trainer says "Paws up" as he or she lifts the dog's front end and guides the dog into position. Instructors often use physical prompting when teaching sports skills, such as how to hold a tennis racket or where to place one's shoulders when playing golf, to people.

Remember that dog training has seen some dramatic changes since the late 1980s, with an emphasis on positive, motivational training. Many obedience instructors and pet-dog trainers do not like the idea of physically placing dogs into position while teaching new skills. These trainers believe that using food or toys to guide dogs into place is the best technique for teaching new skills.

There are some trainers who prefer to physically prompt dogs that are being taught new skills. This technique has been around for decades, and many trainers feel comfortable using the techniques that they know best. Hopefully, these trainers will also choose to learn new methods and will select the best method for any given dog.

If you decide to use physical prompting to teach a skill, make sure that you know the dog well, you have previously handled him a lot, you don't use excessive force, and you feel confident that the dog won't mind being touched and physically moved.

Guiding the dog into position can be a particularly useful technique for dogs that are not responsive to food or toys. Some shelter dogs could not care less about taking food from someone during a training session. Dogs that have been abused or neglected and dogs that are not well socialized can also fall into this category. When presented with food during a training session, these aloof dogs stand with blank looks on their faces as if to say, "I have no interest in your silly treats."

There are also individual dogs within some breeds that are not very responsive to food and toys used as lures or reinforcers. Chow Chows and Shar-Pei come to mind as examples of breeds that may be unimpressed with training treats and toys. Retired racing Greyhounds sometimes refuse to accept food during training, as do individual dogs of several other breeds. Remember, if you decide to use physical prompting, be sure that you know the dog well and that he has a history of tolerating touch.

To teach your dog to sit using physical prompts, follow these steps:

1. Follow the suggestions outlined in the first step of Method 1. Get yourself ready, make sure you have about twenty minutes for training, and get your dog's leash and collar. You can use food rewards with this method, although this technique is often used with dogs that do not accept food.

2. With this method, you won't be in front of the dog; you'll be on one side so that you can get your hands on him. Choose the side on which you want the dog to work. Remember, if you want to do any formal training beyond CGC, you'll want to teach

your dog to work on your left side. If you are right-handed, you may find it easier to physically prompt the dog if he is on your left side. If you are left-handed and find it awkward to use physical prompting with the dog on your left side, you can teach the skill with the dog on your right side and then move the dog to your left side once he knows it well.

Dogs who pass the CGC Test have a good foundation for further training and the opportunity to earn advanced titles.

3. Stand with your dog on leash at your left side. Hold the leash in your right hand. (Reverse these directions if training with the dog on your right side.)

4. With one coordinated, graceful motion in which you do several things at once, pull up (straight up toward the ceiling) gently on the leash with your right hand as you bend over or squat beside the dog, put your left arm/hand behind the dog's back legs, and, with a scooping motion, help the dog into a sit. As the dog's rear end is being lowered into the sit position, say "Sit."

5. For some dogs, variations on this technique might work a little better. For example, for a very calm dog with whom you do not need to use the leash for control, place your right hand on the dog's chest as you guide his rear end into a sit and say "Sit."

6. You might see a beginning trainer doing what comes naturally as he tries to teach the sit. The trainer wants the dog's rear end to go down, so he begins pushing on the rear end. Do not do this. While you may get to the point where you can lightly pat the dog as a reminder to sit, pushing down on the rear end could cause harm to the dog's hips and legs. This is especially dangerous for puppies.

7. The instant that the dog is in the sit position, enthusiastically say "Good sit!" You want to get in the habit of praising your dog as he is learning new skills. For a dog that is not very responsive to social praise, you can tone down the enthusiasm but continue to praise the dog to indicate to him that he performed the skill correctly.

8. When you get the dog to the point that, by using the physical prompting described in Step 4, he sits quickly, you can begin to phase out your assistance. Give a very

light tug on the leash and very lightly touch the backs of his legs as a prompt. Praise when he sits. Gradually phase out the prompts until your dog can sit without you touching him and when you simply say "Sit."

9. Now that your dog will sit on cue, you're ready to move around and add time in between the sit commands. Instruct the dog to sit, then just step off to the side and have the dog get out of the sitting position and walk with you on leash. If your dog likes petting, you can give him a pat and say "Good boy, let's go," to indicate that you are taking a short break. Remember that a training session should be about twenty minutes long, but this is not intended to be twenty minutes of one sit right after the other. You might do five sit attempts and then give the dog a short break during which you keep him on leash and walk around in a small area, pet him, and then announce "OK, let's work." Repeat this sequence a few times over the course of a twenty-minute session.

10. After the dog can sit on your left side when you give the verbal cue "Sit," practice the skill with your dog on the right side, with you standing in front of your dog, and with you standing several feet (about a meter) away from your dog.

Tolerating Petting

Your dog has learned to sit. You've also been practicing meeting strangers, and in your daily playtime, you've been handling your dog a lot. If you have a small dog or a puppy, sitting on the floor with him and tickling, hugging, cuddling, and playing with toys have resulted in a lot of fun, but these games do far more than simply provide you and your dog with a good time. They also build a bond and get your dog accustomed to being handled.

The next step is to ask other people to pet your dog. When the dog tolerates petting and has learned to sit on cue, it's time to combine the two skills. Ask a friend to help you. Have your dog sit at your side on leash. Initially, your friend can approach, say hello to you and the dog, briefly pet the dog, and then back up. Over time, increase the duration of petting until your dog will sit at your side and tolerate a minute or so of petting.

PET HIM LIKE THIS—A LESSON FOR PEOPLE

As a responsible dog owner, you have assumed the responsibility of keeping your dog safe and making him feel comfortable and unafraid when out in the world. However, sometimes people, even those who really love dogs, don't have a clue about how to approach them. You may have gone to a park with your dog and experienced what happens when a group of excited, wound-up children notices that there is a dog nearby. "Oooh, look at the dog!" shouts one, setting off squeals and more loud exclamations: "Hey, doggy! Look at the pretty dog!" And then here they come, running at you and your dog.

As a responsible dog owner, this would be a good time for you to say, "Don't run—that scares my dog—but you can walk up quietly if you'd like to pet him." Sometime, somewhere, somehow, people (children and adults alike) got the strange idea that dogs like to have unfamiliar hands quickly approach to give them hard, quick, repeated pats on the head. Where did this come from? While some dogs can tolerate this, others don't like it one bit (can you blame them?). A dog may be fearful of petting that comes in the form of a hand coming down over his head and eyes.

You should feel free to educate people before they start petting your dog. Tell the person how your dog likes to be petted: "Please pet him under the chin," or "He prefers that you scratch his chest." Some breeds are particularly sensitive about vigorous petting, while some larger breeds don't respond well to head pats. A number of breeds (and individual dogs) often don't welcome hands coming over the tops of their heads because they can't see what is coming. Unless a dog is very social and initiates interaction, it is a good idea to let dogs acclimate to you before petting.

A WORD ABOUT GREYHOUNDS: WITH TRAINING, SIT HAPPENS

We hear it all the time at the American Kennel Club: "I have a retired racing Greyhound, and everyone knows Greyhounds can't sit. My dog needs an exception on the CGC Test." With proper training, all dogs, and that includes Greyhounds, can learn to sit. Sitting may not be the preferred position for these regal hounds, but they can certainly learn to sit for the few moments required in the CGC Test.

Greyhounds can be taught to sit using Method 2, discussed earlier in this chapter. With your right hand on the dog's chest and your left hand sliding down his rear legs to tuck the dog into position, you can put your "standing room only" Greyhound into a sit position. Likewise, many trainers who work with Greyhounds (and other large dogs) use food to guide the dogs into the sit position (Method 1). However, instead of starting with the dog standing, many Greyhound trainers suggest using the food to guide the dog into the down position (see CGC Test Item 6: Sit and Down on Command/Staying in Place). Once the dog is in the down position, you can use food to lure him up into a sit position.

In a survey of CGC Evaluators, the majority of those who responded to the survey said that they teach Greyhounds to first sit on a mat or rug, then the mat is eventually faded.

These rescued retired racing Greyhounds were all taught to sit by Cynda Crawford, PhD, DVM. Dr. Crawford trained the dogs so they could work as therapy dogs and compete in obedience after they were adopted.

It's much easier and more enjoyable to greet and pet a dog when the dog is sitting at the owner's side.

Teaching Puppies to Sit for Petting

When it's time to teach sitting politely for petting, active puppies can present a challenge to trainers in the form of wiggling, wiggling, and more wiggling. There is a lot of joy associated with puppyhood. The tendency for puppies to act excited when meeting people is developmental and should not be viewed as a problem.

When teaching a puppy to sit politely for petting, set small, manageable goals; move forward very slowly; and plan training and activities that are fun and reinforcing. Don't try to get your puppy enrolled in college before he's had time for preschool!

What Comes Next?

After you combine sitting on command, tolerating petting, and sitting politely for petting, expand your dog's social skills by adding variations on these exercises:

- In formal obedience and conformation, your dog will stand for an examination by a judge. In Novice A obedience, in the first exercise that the dog will have to perform, the judge walks up to the dog and touches his head, shoulders, and back (near the tail). Give these exercises a try with a helper and see how your dog does.
- The ultimate version of this skill is to have your dog sit to meet people who come into your home or in the community. For some dogs, this could take several months of practice.
- Give your dog the chance to sit for petting at places like the veterinarian's office, the pet-supply store, and other dog-friendly locations in the community.

APPEARANCE AND GROOMING

This practical test demonstrates that the dog will welcome being groomed and examined and will permit a stranger, such as a veterinarian, groomer, or friend of the owner, to do these tasks. This test also demonstrates the owner's care, concern, and sense of responsibility.

The Evaluator inspects the dog to determine if he is clean and groomed. The dog must appear to be in healthy condition (i.e., at a proper weight, clean, healthy, and alert). The handler should supply the comb or brush that he or she commonly uses on the dog at home. The Evaluator softly combs or brushes the dog and, in a natural manner, lightly examines the dog's ears and gently picks up each front foot.

- It is not necessary for the dog to hold a specific position during the examination, and the handler may talk to the dog, praise him, and give him encouragement.
- The Evaluator may give the handler specific instructions for handling the dog in a manner that ensures safety. For example, when the feet are to be handled, the Evaluator may request that the handler lift each leg. The Evaluator may request that the handler steady the dog's head while the Evaluator checks the ears.
- Another technique the Evaluator may use is to hold the dog's head away with one hand and use the other hand to lift the foot.
- While the Evaluator may ask the handler to steady the dog's head, lift a leg, etc., any dog requiring someone to restrain him for examination should not pass the test. The key question for this test is, "Could a veterinarian or groomer easily examine the dog?"
- Some dogs will wiggle or squirm when they are excited. Some squirming is acceptable; however, it should not be so excessive that the dog cannot be brushed.
- The dog should not struggle (pull away with intensity) to avoid being brushed.

A well-groomed dog will surely be an attention-getter. CGC Test Item 3, Appearance and Grooming, shows that a dog will welcome an inspection from a person other than the owner.

There's nothing that will turn heads quite like a clean, healthy, nicely groomed dog that has been well cared for. This dog is maintained at a proper weight for his age and breed and has good muscle tone acquired by regular exercise. This canine show-stopper is a happy-looking dog with a coat that shines and eyes that sparkle.

In CGC Test Item 3, Appearance and Grooming, the Evaluator will brush your dog and touch his feet and ears. In the real world, you'll want to expand these CGC skills into the full range of grooming tasks performed by you or a professional groomer. This chapter will show you how.

Happy, Healthy Appearance

Let's talk about appearance first. When we say "appearance" in CGC, we're not talking about being pretty or handsome or having attractive markings. We're referring to the overall good appearance that results when a dog is healthy.

Appearance as addressed in the CGC Test means that dogs are not seriously underweight or overweight. Underweight dogs could need more food or a different diet, they could have some form of parasites, or they could have health problems that need medical attention. If your dog is significantly underweight, as a responsible owner, you should address the problem with your veterinarian. Being overweight can also prevent dogs from being as healthy as possible. A dog that is overweight may be getting too much food, the wrong kind of food, or too little exercise, or there could be a medical problem that needs treatment. If you love your dog so much that you can't say no when it comes to food, you could be unintentionally hurting his health.

Also related to general appearance is your dog's skin and coat. The skin and coat are good visual indicators of a dog's health. The skin should not be dry or flaking, nor should it be excessively oily. The skin should be free from sores, rashes, and inflammation. An inspection of a healthy dog's coat will reveal that there are no parasites, such as fleas or ticks. A healthy dog's coat is not dull or dry. A healthy coat has a shine to it and is not overly oily. Additionally, the dog's eyes are clear, and there is no discharge coming from his eyes or nose.

The Evaluator may talk to and encourage the dog during the examination.

Good Grooming Practices

Grooming is the key to maintaining a healthy appearance. Learning to groom your dog can be a rewarding activity that both your dog and you can come to enjoy. If this is your first dog, you may need some help learning the fundamentals.

A great place to learn how to keep your dog looking his best is your local AKC-affiliated dog club. The AKC has nearly 5,000 clubs across the United States, and in these clubs you'll find new friends who are eager to share their knowledge and experience.

If you have a breed such as the Poodle that requires a great deal of specialized grooming, you can join a specialty club. Specialty clubs are for one breed only, so in this type of club you'll find a whole group of people who own your breed.

If the time in your life isn't right to join a club, attend meetings, and participate in activities, another option is to simply contact the club to get the name of a club member who might be willing to meet with you once or twice to teach you how to groom your dog. Most dog lovers are thrilled to have an opportunity to help someone learn to give his or her dog better care. To find AKC clubs near you, go to *www.akc.org* and type "Clubs" in the search box.

A well-groomed dog has an overall look of good health.

Preparation Exercises for Appearance and Grooming

Remember the exercises and games we recommended for teaching your puppy or new dog to tolerate petting? The daily handling, petting, and massaging of your dog during your playtime sessions lays the groundwork for teaching a dog to tolerate grooming.

Brushing and Combing Your Dog

One of the easiest grooming tasks is brushing your dog. Brushing stimulates the release and distribution of oil in the coat to give it a shine. Brushing is also important because it removes dirt from the dog's coat.

With a puppy or newly acquired adult dog, begin by making sure that the dog is comfortable with the brush. Start by just showing it to him. Put the brush on the floor and let the dog sniff it. Next, start brushing gently. Many dogs instantly love being brushed and will drop to the floor and roll over as if to say, "Right here on my tummy, please."

If you have a dog that is afraid of the brush, start with short sessions. Begin by touching the dog with the brush, then adding a stroke or two, and eventually progressing to brushing one area of the body.

Depending on your dog's coat type, you may need a special kind of brush. There are brushing mitts that are worn like gloves and work very well with flat-coated dogs. The following section on brushing and combing describes other special grooming tools, such as slickers, rakes, and stripping knives.

Desensitizing Your Dog to Equipment

Most dogs love the tactile stimulation that comes with brushing and grooming; with these dogs, you can jump right in with brushing, bathing, and other beauty routines. But some dogs, especially those that were not exposed to grooming as puppies, have a problem with being groomed and are afraid of the equipment. Desensitization is the best procedure

If you brush your dog regularly, he will in turn accept being brushed by others.

Taking the time to desensitize your dog to grooming items will reduce the risk of fearful reactions to brushes and other equipment.

for dealing with a grooming problem, such as fear of equipment or resistance to having a particular body part touched.

You've probably heard the saying "one step at a time." That's the idea behind desensitization, which is a procedure that involves slowly introducing your dog to something new by first presenting a stimulus that is less problematic than your ultimate goal. For example, let's say that your dog is very fearful of being brushed. You get out the brush and immediately attempt to brush his face, but you can't because the dog has started to spin around, back up, and pull away. You have visions of your dog plastered to the ceiling like a cartoon character. To try desensitization, do the following:

1. Select the brush you will use. Put it on the floor beside the dog, then pick up the brush and let the dog smell it.
2. When the dog is comfortable with the brush, show the brush to the dog, lightly touch it to his hindquarters, and slowly begin to brush. Don't start with his face, feet, or other sensitive areas.
3. When you can brush the dog's back end (including the upper parts of the legs and his back near the tail), try brushing the dog's back in sections until you can start at the neck and brush all the way to the tail.
4. After you can brush your dog's back, move on to the chest.
5. Next, you're ready for the head, the face, and finally the feet. Be gentle when brushing these sensitive parts of the body.

Handling the Feet

In your daily bonding sessions in which you sit on the floor with your pup or dog for games, hugging, and petting, you should be handling his feet. In an ideal world, puppies are given plenty of handling from the time they are born. A part of that handling includes touching the feet and toes so that the puppies are ready for routine grooming and care.

If you haven't started this already, begin by simply touching each foot, progressing to the point at which you can handle each foot for several seconds, look between the toes, and touch each nail. Not only is handling the feet good preparation for clipping nails and trimming the hair on the feet, it also gives you a chance to make sure that your dog has not picked up a thorn or developed any sores between the pads of his feet.

If your dog has sensitive feet, you can do a desensitization program that focuses on the feet.

1. If your dog's feet are sensitive, start by handling the upper leg, near the shoulder. Pet, brush, or massage the area.
2. Slowly (this may take a few sessions) move your hand down the dog's leg. Can you touch or brush the leg halfway between the shoulder and foot? When you can do this, continue to pet, massage, or brush closer to the foot.
3. For dogs that have a major problem with having their feet touched, treats can be used during desensitization to make sessions more rewarding.
4. Finally, holding the dog in a safe, secure position can prevent an accident with the clippers or grinder, and it can help calm the dog.

Bathing

Grooming should begin with a clean coat, which means you'll need to give your dog a bath using the proper equipment. This includes a nonslip surface, warm water, a leash and collar until your dog is very reliable with the stay cue, treats for shaping good behavior, and a no-sting dog shampoo.

Take some time to research the different shampoos available for dogs. There are specialty shampoos for cleaning tear stains from the faces of white dogs, hypoallergenic shampoos, shampoos designed to make light coats brighter and dark coats darker, shampoos for curly coats, shampoos for wiry coats, shampoos for various skin problems, flea- and tick-repellent shampoos, shampoos that make your dog smell nice, and on and on.

Depending on your dog's coat type, you might also need a good conditioner to help reduce mats and "frizzies," thereby ensuring that your dog will always have a good hair day (even if you don't!). Towels and hair dryers (there are dryers designed for dogs, but those made for humans will work just fine) will dry the coat. And one more thing—until you and your dog have the hang of the bathing routine, you may want to wear waterproof clothes!

So it's time for a bath. Now what?

- ❧ Decide where you will bathe your dog. If you have a small dog, you can bathe him in a laundry sink, a kitchen sink, or a small tub, thereby saving your back. Medium-sized and large dogs can be bathed in a bathtub or, when the temperature is suitable, outside with the garden hose.

- ❧ If you have a long-coated dog, make sure that there are no mats or tangles in his coat before bathing. Always give the dog a thorough brushing before starting the bath.

- ❧ Which end is up? When wetting and shampooing a dog, some people will tell you to start with the head and work toward the back. Others will tell you to start at the back and work toward the head. Either way will get the dog clean. If you live in an area where your dog may get the occasional flea, start at the head. You don't want to start at the rear end of the dog, because the fleas will scurry to hide in the dog's ears. If you have a timid dog that does not like getting his head and face wet, start at the rear and work forward. This way, you'll save the worst for last, and bath time will be over after a quick wash of the face and head.

- ❧ Use warm water to thoroughly wet the dog. When the dog is wet, begin applying the shampoo and massaging it into a good, soapy lather. Go over every area of the dog, making sure to work the shampoo into the coat. Don't get shampoo in the dog's eyes or ears. If you need to, you can put a cotton ball in each ear to keep the water out.

- ❧ When your dog is clean, rinse until there is no more soap in the water. If you've chosen to use a conditioner, follow the instructions on the bottle and apply it before you dry the dog.

- Your dog will likely attempt to shake the water out of his coat after a bath. This gives you a good head start on drying the dog! Use a towel to get much of the remaining water out of the coat.
- For a dog with thicker fur or a longer coat, you can use a handheld hair dryer to blow-dry the coat. With a fearful dog, you might need to use desensitization to get him accustomed to the noise of the hair dryer. Pay close attention to the temperature when using a hair dryer to prevent damaging the coat or, worse, accidentally burning your dog. Some commercial dryers designed for dogs produce a lot of heat and should always be used with close supervision—never put your dog in a crate under the dryer and leave the area. This lapse in judgment can result in a disaster, particularly for brachycephalic (flat-faced) breeds, such as Bulldogs, Pugs, and Pekingese.

Cleaning the Ears

In the Appearance and Grooming exercise, the Evaluator lightly examines the dog's ears. Touching and handling the ears is the first step in the chain of grooming tasks that will prevent your dog from getting ear infections or parasites in the ears. A few simple tips will help you keep your dog's ears clean, dry, and free of infections or mites. If you have any questions about your ear-cleaning technique, ask your vet, a vet tech, or an experienced groomer for a quick lesson.

Routine ear care can prevent your dog from getting infections or parasites in the ears.

1. After you can touch and handle your dog's ears, move on to a more thorough exam. Start with one ear. Hold the ear in your hand, looking at and feeling the outside of it. Do you see any bumps, scratches, or other problems? Do the same with the other ear.
2. Next, check inside the ears. If the ears are dirty, use a clean cloth or cotton ball to clean them. You can moisten the cloth or cotton with ear wash (available at a pet-supply store or from your vet) or a little water and then gently remove the dirt or wax. If the ear has a lot of dirt or wax, you can use alcohol or mineral oil.

3. If there is any foul odor coming from your dog's ears or you've noticed your dog shaking his head, it could be mites or an infection, and you should have your veterinarian check the ears as soon as possible.

4. Dogs with heavier coats may have a lot of hair growing inside their ears. If the opening to your dog's ear canal is blocked with hair, some of the hair needs to be trimmed. Be extremely careful when trimming hair in or around the ears because there are many small folds that you can accidentally cut. A good safety technique for beginning groomers is to hold the hair between the thumb and index finger and cut the hair that protrudes from the tops of the fingers.

5. Groomers often pluck the hair out of dogs' ears using forceps. Before you try this for the first time, make sure you have someone demonstrate how to do it. Groomers also use clippers on the insides of the ears of some dogs with long ears, such as spaniels. Clippers should be used with care, and it is a good idea to have someone teach you how to use them.

Brushing and Combing Equipment

In the Appearance and Grooming CGC Test Item, the Evaluator will softly brush or comb the dog. As mentioned, you'll bring your own brush, comb, or grooming mitt to the test, and, ideally, you will have selected your tool based on your dog's coat type. There are various tools of the trade for brushing or combing your dog. Most common include a pin brush, bristle brush, comb, and rake.

Owners will bring their dogs' own brushes or combs to the CGC Test. Long-coated dogs will usually be brushed, while owners might bring grooming mitts for flat-coated dogs.

Typically, pin brushes are used on dogs with medium to long coats. The pins pull through the coat, separating it, cleaning out dirt, and eliminating small tangles.

Bristle brushes can be used on shorter coats and on faces. They can also be used as the last step in brushing to smooth the coat and make a dog "picture perfect." Back in the day, young girls were told to brush their hair for at least 100 strokes a day to keep it looking healthy and shiny. The bristle brush is that 100-strokes-a-day brush that can be used to keep your dog's coat looking good. Your dog will love it if you sit on the floor with him while watching your favorite TV show and give him a good brushing with a bristle brush.

Combs are good for grooming dogs with short or very fine hair. You don't want to drag a comb through a long, heavy coat. Combs are good for straightening and arranging short hair and removing debris. In areas where there are fleas, special flea combs can be used to remove these pests from the dog. The teeth of a flea comb are very close together so that something as small as a flea can be easily removed.

A grooming rake looks like a very small version of your basic garden rake, with a handle and a row of teeth. A rake is an excellent tool for pulling out dead undercoat. Used on a breed such as the Siberian Husky, which has a heavy undercoat, a rake can painlessly pull out enough undercoat to knit a sweater! With the dead undercoat removed, the dog's coat can breathe, and, as an added benefit, you'll have much less shed hair to vacuum. A rake can also be used to split up tangles and mats in the coat.

Other brushing tools include rubber brushes, grooming mitts (as mentioned earlier, gloves with texturized palms, usually used on flat coats), curry brushes (oval-shaped rings of metal or rubber attached to a handle), and slicker brushes (very fine, soft metal teeth mounted in soft rubber on a handle). These tools are all used to neaten a dog's appearance, loosen mats, and remove unwanted hair.

To brush your dog, begin with one section at a time. For example, start with one back leg and gradually move to the second back leg, then the belly, and so on. If the dog has a long or thick coat, don't simply run the brush over the top of the coat. Doing this may make the top of the coat look nice, but you will only cover up tangles underneath.

Work in sections of a few inches (7 to 8 centimeters) each, holding up the hair and carefully brushing each section. If you find a tangle, don't just force the brush through the tangle. Hold the tangle by placing your fingers between the tangle and the dog's body. This method prevents the painful pulling of hair that will quickly cause the dog to no longer tolerate brushing.

Haircuts

If you have a "wash-and-wear" dog, such as a German Shorthaired Pointer or a Doberman Pinscher, you won't have many hairstyle choices to make. If you have a dog with a fuller or longer coat, you will have some grooming options to think about. For example, do you want your Poodle to be clipped in one of the standard cuts for the breed? If so, you can either refer to a book that shows you how to do Poodle clips, learn from another Poodle owner, or have a professional groomer clip your dog's hair for you. If you've adopted a shaggy terrier mix from the shelter, he would look adorable with a Schnauzer cut.

Think about your lifestyle and which haircut will be best for your dog. An Old English Sheepdog has hair over his eyes in the conformation ring, but you may want to cut this hair (or, at the minimum, use barrettes) if your dog is competing in agility. In the show ring, your English Springer Spaniel looks great with a full coat and belly hair that goes nearly to the floor, but a shorter cut may be better for a family pet that has retired from competition and enjoys a daily swim in the pool.

The most common tools you'll need for giving your dog a stylish canine cut include scissors, thinning shears, and, with some breeds, electric clippers. If you choose to use clippers, make sure you get some training from an experienced person so that you'll know which blade is best for your dog.

Foot and Nail Care

As with humans, dogs need proper care of their feet and nails. The feet of heavily coated breeds should appear neat. This is for more than cosmetic reasons. When the hair between the footpads is trimmed, air can circulate better, and the dog is less likely to get infections.

Professional groomers use clippers to trim between a dog's toes. However, this takes skill and practice. If you have a well-trained dog that will hold still while you groom his feet, you can use scissors to clip the hair on the bottom of the feet and between the toes.

As for the nails, it is surprising how many experienced dog trainers have trouble clipping their dogs' nails. Rather than dealing with a dog that goes berserk when he sees the nail clippers, some owners will have the dog's nails clipped by a groomer or veterinarian throughout the dog's entire life. Training your dog to accept nail care early in his life not only makes your life easier but also could save you a lot of money.

If you have trouble clipping your dog's nails, don't despair. This is a skill you can learn. The first step is to make sure that you can handle the dog's feet. Positive motivational procedures combined with desensitization, as we discussed earlier, are the trick to being able to handle ticklish paws.

Nail clippers come in several varieties; the most well-known types are the scissor-style clippers and the guillotine clippers. For a little more money, there are safety clippers with a lighted sensor that tells you when you are getting too close to the inner part of the nail, called the *quick*, which contains sensitive nerves and blood vessels. To prevent cutting the quick when using clippers, be conservative and take off only a small piece at a time.

A grinder is another helpful tool for shortening your dog's nails. The grinder is a handheld tool with a grinding bit that is covered with a sandpaper-like surface. If you are disciplined about maintaining your dog's nails regularly, the grinder may be all that you need, and you can avoid having to use clippers. However, the grinder heats up during use, so don't risk burning your dog by using a grinder on overly long nails. Nail clipping is another task for which we recommend some hands-on training from a knowledgeable person.

Selecting a Groomer

You might have a breed with a coat that depends on advanced grooming skills to look its absolute best. Or you might be very busy, and you'd like to have someone else groom your dog. Good news! There are professional groomers who are ready and waiting to provide this service to you. You can find a groomer online, through recommendations from dog-owning friends or your veterinarian, or at a local pet-supply store.

The nature of grooming is such that if your dog has a bad experience with a groomer or grooming equipment, it can result in his being very fearful for a long time. For this reason, when you are selecting a groomer, ask about the person's training and skills. If you have a breed that requires a particular style or clip, find out if the groomer has ever worked on your breed.

It's a good idea to ask if the groomer would be willing to let you observe from a distance as he grooms a dog. The groomers at many large pet-supply stores work behind large windows so that customers can observe.

Take a close look at your dog after his first visit to a new groomer. Are you happy with the results of all services provided? Also pay attention to how your dog responds to the groomer. A dog should not be traumatized when he visits the groomer. When you observe, you should not see anyone hitting or otherwise being rough with dogs that squirm and act fearful.

More Than Just a Test Item

Your dog's appearance and grooming will be important throughout the life of your dog, not just for the CGC Test. Grooming goes far beyond making your dog look nice—it plays an important role in keeping your dog's skin, coat, eyes, ears, and feet healthy and problem-free.

Beginning when your dog is a puppy, practicing specifically for the CGC Test will help desensitize him to grooming equipment and routines. As you work with your dog, think of the functional aspect of this test item, which was intended to produce a dog that accepts grooming and routine veterinary checkups without conflict.

Working on additional exercises toward this goal is a good idea. For example, even though it is not on the CGC Test, you should also check your dog's mouth, much like a veterinarian would do. Regular brushing with special toothpaste made for dogs will keep his teeth clean and prevent gum disease.

Also remember that exposing a puppy to grooming tasks early in his life will result in a dog that looks forward to grooming. With a dog that is getting a late start, sound behavioral procedures such as desensitization and positive reinforcement can be used to teach the dog to tolerate grooming.

Finally, tactile stimulation—touch—can be a very powerful reinforcer for both humans and animals. With regular practice, your dog will soon welcome grooming time with you. Passing Test Item 3 of the Canine Good Citizen Test demonstrates that your dog is compliant, under control, and well cared for.

When preparing your dog for the Appearance and Grooming Test Item, he will learn the important life lesson that he can trust you and other people to handle him with care.

OUT FOR A WALK
(WALKING ON A LOOSE LEASH)

This test demonstrates that the handler is in control of the dog when out for a walk. The dog may be on either side of the handler, whichever the handler prefers. (**Note:** The left-side position is required in AKC obedience competitions.)

The Evaluator may use a preplanned course or may direct the handler by calling out instructions (e.g., "right turn"). Whichever format is used, there must be a right turn, left turn, and about turn, with at least one stop in between and one at the end.

The handler may talk to the dog throughout the "walk" to encourage him and may also praise him. The handler may also give the dog a command to sit when they stop, if desired.

- The dog's position should leave no doubt that the dog is attentive to the handler and is responding to the handler's movements and changes of direction.
- The dog need not be perfectly aligned with the handler and need not sit at the stops.
- The dog should not be constantly straining at the leash so that the leash is pulled tight. The Evaluator may instruct the handler to loosen (put more slack in) the leash. An occasional tight leash may be permitted.
- Excessive sniffing of the floor or ground, such that the dog will not walk along with the handler, should result in the dog not passing the test.
- If the dog is totally inattentive to the handler (e.g., does not change directions), he should not pass the test.

Walking

As soon as someone decides to get a dog, he or she starts to imagine taking that wonderful new dog for a walk. Full of great anticipation and excitement, the person imagines exactly how it will go. With the perfect puppy on a thoughtfully selected, attractive new leash, they will walk down the sidewalk together

Daily walks offer significant benefits for owners, dogs, and their relationship with each other. A dog should be under control when taking a walk in the CGC Test, in the neighborhood, or at a public event where dogs are welcome.

with pride. Everyone will stop to pet the dog and compliment the owner, the sun will be shining, the birds will be singing, and there will be happy music playing in the background.

Sometimes, though, it doesn't turn out like this. Instead, like an escapee from the Iditarod, the excited, active dog pulls on the leash with great strength, dragging the owner down the street. And don't think for one minute that large and medium-sized dogs are the only culprits when it comes to wrecking a walk. Small dogs that pull also make walking them unpleasant. Because of their speed and small size, they can wrap the leash around their owners' legs before you can say "training." After coming home from several walks with leash marks embedded in the palms of both hands from a large dog's pulling, or a serious case of embarrassment over a total inability to control a 6-pound ball of fur, you may decide that your dog can get all of the exercise he needs in the backyard. When this happens, both you and the dog lose.

Item 4 of the Canine Good Citizen Test is Out for a Walk (Walking on a Loose Leash). For big dogs, we say this is the "your arm should not be pulled out of the socket" test. The ability to walk nicely on a leash increases the dog's chances that his owner will

This Great Dane has the horsepower to drag someone down the street, but thanks to Canine Good Citizen training, this canine companion is calm and controlled.

want to take him for walks. When daily walks becomes part of the routine, dog and owner get fresh air, exercise, and the significant benefit of bonding with each other.

It's true that a dog can get plenty of exercise in a large fenced backyard. However, what our canine companions get on walks that even the largest yard doesn't provide is socialization with other dogs and people. When a dog is taken for walks in the community, he not only gets exercise but also is exposed to new stimuli and experiences, which are critical for developing the dog's intelligence and emotional well-being. This chapter provides tips for teaching your dog to walk on a loose leash.

Starting Position

In the CGC Test, handlers may walk with their dogs on the left or right side, whichever is preferred. Unless you have a disability, we suggest that you train your dog to work on your left side. As mentioned earlier, this is the side required in AKC competitive events (accommodations are made for handlers with disabilities) to ensure that the exercises are standardized. For example, when you walk in a circle with a dog at your left side, if you circle to the right, the dog is on the outside. If you go to the left, it becomes a completely different exercise with the dog on the inside.

We've also mentioned that the tradition of dogs working on their handlers' left sides began in the early days of hunting, as most people are right-handed and would have had their guns in their right hands and their dogs on their left sides. Further, when handlers walked with dogs and horses together, the horses were typically on the right and the dogs on the left. We're hoping that you'll get hooked on training while

Working with your dog on the left side will prepare you for activities such as competitive obedience.

preparing for the CGC Test, and working with your dog on your left side will prepare both of you for training for and competing in fun events such as Rally and obedience.

Teaching Out for a Walk
Using Food or a Toy as a Lure

* Use a toy to play with your dog and establish the toy as a reinforcer (something the dog wants and will work to earn). You can also do this with a preferred treat.
* Start with your dog at your side.
* Hold the lure in your hand (at the center of your waist).
* Walk forward as you give the verbal command you've chosen, such as walk or heel. It's a good idea to start working on heel now, although your dog does not have to be in the heel position during the CGC Test.
* When the dog starts to walk along with you, praise him ("Good dog!").
* Periodically give the dog the treat or toy as a reward for walking nicely on the leash. In the beginning, you will use the reward more often and will eventually phase out the food or toy. Your praise, along with the enjoyment of going for a walk, will eventually be the reward.

- Start with short distances, walking in a straight line. During your training, begin with ten to fifteen steps and then gradually lengthen the distance.
- When your dog walks well on leash in a straight line, add unusual patterns such as walking in circles (both clockwise and counterclockwise), weaving in and out of objects, making quick turns to the left and right, and stopping. Eventually, you should teach your dog to sit when you stop.

Advanced Exercise: Heeling

One trick to teach the dog to work close to your left side is to start in a hallway or along the outside of a long building. Put the dog on your left side against the wall and say "Heel" as you begin to move forward. The wall keeps the dog in position.

To teach heeling in an open room or outdoor area, do the following:

- Begin with the dog sitting on your left side. Have small bits of food rewards in your right hand.
- Step off with your left foot as you say "Heel." The reason for stepping off on your left foot every time is that the dog can easily pick up on the motion of the left leg (which is beside him) moving forward. Eventually, you will be able to start walking without any verbal cues, and the dog will respond to your consistent body cues.

Purebred and mixed-breed dogs of any size can excel at CGC training. In the CGC Test, the dog does not have to be in the heel position required in formal obedience. Here, the dog is slightly behind the owner, but the leash is loose, so the dog would pass the test.

- ✿ Keeping your body (shoulders and trunk) facing forward, walk along for a few steps, praising the dog for being in the heel position ("Good dog, heel!"). If you are training with food, you can also give a food reward every few steps in the very beginning of training. Brisk walking is a good way to get the dog moving forward. When you are slow and tentative, the dog may not get the message that the point of heeling is to move along beside you.
- ✿ After several steps, stop by taking your last step on your right foot, then bring your left foot in next to your right foot. Your dog should stop walking.
- ✿ You can also work on having the dog sit each time you stop.
- ✿ Repeat the process until your dog will heel nicely in a long straight line, then add other patterns (left turn, right turn, circles, about turn).
- ✿ Have your dog heel in a place where there are distractions, such as children playing nearby, other people walking by, and so on.

Techniques to Stop Pulling on the Leash

If your dog pulls on the leash, and you allow him to pull you along, you've reinforced him for pulling. He got what he wanted, which was the forward motion he needed to get to another dog or a great new smell, and, if you allow him to do this once, he will do it again. Don't reward the dog (albeit unintentionally) for pulling!

Technique 1

1. When he starts to pull, stop walking.
2. Stand still. Don't move forward with the dog.
3. Wait. The dog will pull, but eventually he'll stop.
4. When he stops pulling, you can praise him and move forward. *Uh-oh*. He is so excited that you're moving forward, he's pulling again. Now what?
5. Repeat the procedure. It won't take long until he figures out that you aren't going anywhere as long as he pulls.

Technique 2

1. When your dog begins to go in his own direction, briskly turn and go in the opposite direction. He'll have to come along and will likely hurry to keep up with you.
2. When the dog begins to follow along in the direction in which you are now moving, praise him and, during the beginning stages of training, give him a treat for coming with you. Your dog will soon learn to watch you.

In AKC S.T.A.R. Puppy training, a little food encourages the pup to stay by the owner's side.

Walking Etiquette

As you plan a walk with your dog, you may have a destination in mind. You may be walking around the block, across the park, or to buy something from the world-class bakery on the corner. A part of each walk can certainly involve serious, businesslike walking from point A to point B in which you give an instruction such as "Let's walk."

Remember, though, that walks are also a way for dogs to learn about the neighborhoods in which they live. Part of the time, you may want to let your dog explore new objects or scents. Verbal cues will help the dog distinguish between when he needs to trot along with you and when it is OK to read the local "pee-mail." Verbal cues, such as "Let's walk" and "Free dog" (even though the dog is on leash) help the dog differentiate between walk time and casual sniffing time.

You also have to think about proper etiquette on walks. Just like there are manners for attending tea parties, eating at formal dinners, and responding to e-mail (referred to as *netiquette*), there are manners for taking your dog for a walk.

First and foremost, remember the CGC Responsible Dog Owner's Pledge. In public places, always clean up after your dog. Develop the habit of putting a cleanup bag in your pocket every time you leave for a walk. If you keep a stash of bags near the dog's leash, you'll be

Teaching your dog to pay attention to you is an excellent way to manage your dog on a busy sidewalk, in a hallway, or on a hiking trail.

more likely to reach for one before leaving. You can also purchase a small bag holder that can be refilled with bags and clips onto the leash so that you're always prepared.

Follow the rules. If you see a sign that says "No Dogs," that includes yours. In a large city where there aren't many bathroom areas for dogs, the landscaping in front of a hotel may be tempting, but find somewhere else. In public parks, where areas are designated for wildlife and off-trail use is not permitted, stay on the trails.

Keep in mind that not everyone is a dog lover. On crowded sidewalks, on trails, or in hallways, make sure that you have good control of your dog when someone is approaching. Sometimes moving the dog to your other side will be a good idea. On an elevator, good manners would be putting your dog between yourself and the wall of the elevator so that the dog is not next to people who may not care for animals.

When taking a walk, if a person approaching on the sidewalk also has a dog, keep a close eye on the other dog. If he is pulling or lunging, you may want to have your dog step aside until the person with the unruly dog passes by. Likewise, you also want to make sure that your dog behaves properly in such a situation.

Being polite and using good manners when you take your dog for a walk will help all dog owners retain the right to have dogs in public places. When owners fail to clean up after their dogs, all dog owners suffer. Then, before you know it, dogs have restricted access to the public places in which there have been problems. Walkers, hikers, and people looking for pleasant places for picnics can become extremely vocal about dogs causing problems in public parks. Responsibility begins with you. On every walk you take with your dog, you can set a good example for others.

WALKING THROUGH A CROWD

This test demonstrates that the dog can move about politely in pedestrian traffic and is under control in public places.

The dog and handler walk around and pass close to several (at least three) people. The Evaluator can be counted as one of the three people in the crowd. Children may act as members of the crowd; however, when children participate in the test, they must be instructed on their role and be supervised by an adult. Some of the members of the crowd may be standing still, and some should be moving around. This test simulates settings such as busy sidewalks or walking through a crowd at a public event.

If the CGC Test is being used as a prerequisite to therapy-dog testing and certification, most national therapy-dog groups require that at least one person in the crowd use some healthcare equipment such as walkers, canes, wheelchairs, and the like.

- In this test, the dog may show some interest in the strangers but should continue to walk with the handler without evidence of overexuberance, shyness, or resentment.
- The dog may show mild interest in members of the crowd. The dog may sniff a person in the crowd briefly but must move on promptly.
- The dog may not jump on people in the crowd or attempt to go to them.
- The dog should not be straining on the leash.
- The dog should not be trying to hide behind the handler.

Our dogs adore us and want to spend time with us. Every single one of these devoted, loving creatures deserves a rich life, full of opportunities to accompany their human companions on daily excursions and to special activities. We've already talked about the importance of teaching your dog to walk on a leash. Now it's time to take your canine companion out into the world—you've got places to go and people to meet! Chances are, many of the places you'll go with your dog involve crowds. Busy sidewalks, crowded elevators, the patio at a dog-friendly neighborhood bistro, and public events such as community fairs and dog shows are just some of many places where Test Item 5, Walking through a Crowd, is important.

In the CGC Test, your dog will be tested in a "crowd" of at least three people.

Important Reminders

You're going to teach your dog to mind his manners while in crowds, but during his training, remember that as a responsible owner, there are some things you can do to make others feel better about dog owners.

Using Elevators

When you get onto an elevator with your dog, step to the side if you can, putting the dog between you and the wall. If the elevator is partially full, so that you'll be stepping into the middle space in the front, give your large or medium-sized dog the cue to sit. You can pick up and hold your small dog if you feel it is appropriate to do so. Walking into a small space that is tightly packed with unfamiliar people is unnatural and can be especially frightening for a tiny dog.

Navigating Sidewalks

When walking down a busy sidewalk, you can decide to step aside to allow someone with an out-of-control dog to pass, or, as long as the approaching dog does not appear to be aggressive, you can keep right on walking as a training exercise for your dog.

If your dog is a social butterfly and likes to say hello with his front paws, be aware of this. Until your dog is trained, keep enough distance between the unsuspecting stranger and the "world's friendliest dog" so that the dog can't jump up to give an uninvited greeting.

Problems Related to Walking through a Crowd

In the CGC Test, four of the most common reasons that an Evaluator will score this item as "Needs More Training" are jumping on a person in the crowd, pulling away from the owner to sniff a person in the crowd, reacting in a very fearful way to a person in the crowd, and (infrequently but very unfortunately) urinating on a person in the crowd.

Jumping on People

Jumping on people is a friendly dog's way of saying hello. This is not a behavior problem as much as it is a misguided attempt at canine communication. The dog is excited and eager to meet the person. As far as the dog is concerned, attention from an interesting person would be the absolute best of all possible rewards.

Your first job is to teach the dog to say hello when it is appropriate in an acceptable way (such as to sit nicely to meet a stranger). Your second job is to teach the dog that there are some situations in which we're just going to ignore people and mind our own business (such as when we are walking through a crowd).

The best approach to addressing your dog's jumping on people in a crowd is to work hard to teach your dog to act "on cue" when you say "Heel" or "Let's walk." This is an

In the Urban CGC Test, these dogs demonstrate how to cross the street politely among people and other dogs.

example of the previously mentioned *DRI* (differential reinforcement of incompatible behavior). This means that to solve one problem, such as jumping up, you reward the dog for doing something that is incompatible, such as sit or heel. This is why all of the behaviors on the Canine Good Citizen Test are so important. Behaviors such as sit, down, and stay can be used in many situations to manage unwanted behaviors.

Sniffing People

Another situation that will result in a dog's not passing the Walking through a Crowd part of the Canine Good Citizen Test can be somewhat embarrassing for the owner and the crowd member involved, depending on the specifics of exactly how it occurs. What we're talking about here is when the dog decides to sniff a person in the crowd. If your scent-loving hound takes a quick whiff as he walks by a human, it's usually not a problem. The problem occurs when the dog begins to smell certain areas of the person's body as if to say, "I need to check your name, rank, and serial number." Again, this is simply how canines get information about one another, and the clever dog is simply trying to learn about the people in the crowd.

The trick to preventing this is to teach the dog the heel (or "let's walk") and "leave it" cues. When you are greeting someone outside the CGC Test, the dog can be instructed to sit or lie down.

Fearful of Someone in the Crowd or the Crowd Itself

There are times when a dog might be afraid of a person in a crowd, and this can pertain to a real crowd or the "crowd" in a CGC Test. The trick to dealing with this problem is to provide plenty of socialization. If your dog shows any signs of being afraid of people, you should set up situations for him to meet new human friends. Beginning with quiet, calm people who understand dogs and making the experiences very positive will set the stage for a secure dog that is ready to meet a group of people or a person with a loud voice.

Urinating on a Person in the Crowd

Depending on the individual dog and his personality, there can be a few reasons why a male dog would lift his leg and sprinkle the pants of someone in the crowd. This behavior can be related to dominant dogs that are marking their territory and leaving scent-laden memos for other dogs that will come along later. But what we see most often in the CGC Test are young dogs that are beginning training and may be nervous in new situations. In the middle of the test ring, the nervous male dog feels the need to lift his leg and urinate, and, as it happens, the nearest vertical surface is someone's leg. If this happens, apologize to the person (who will most likely be a sympathetic, experienced dog person who has been there, done that) and move on. Don't yell at your dog or make a big fuss. Practice this test item with friends and family who are willing to act as the crowd.

Teaching Your Dog to Walk through a Crowd

Some owners are dealing with upbeat dogs that have been able to do this exercise with no problems from the day they were born. Other dogs, including dogs that want to greet the crowd and dogs that are afraid in a crowd, need some instruction.

The behavioral technique related to teaching Item 5, Walking through a Crowd, is called *shaping*. Shaping is when you reinforce successive approximations leading to a desired behavior. For example, if you wanted your dog to walk through a crowd of fifteen people, you would start by making sure that the dog could walk close to one person, then two, then five, and so on. Shaping in this exercise can be related to (1) the dog's proximity to the people in the crowd, (2) the number of people in the crowd, or (3) the unfamiliar characteristics (raincoats, wheelchairs) of the people in the crowd.

In some situations, we want our dogs to interact with others, but in most situations when walking through a crowd, the dog should ignore other people.

- Start by having your dog walk, on a leash, past one person who is 10 feet (3m) away. When the dog can do this with no problems, get closer.
- Have the dog walk past a person who is 5 feet (1.5m) away. The dog should not be pulling to go to the person. If necessary, remind your dog with "Watch me" or "Heel." Praise the dog for walking along with you.
- Have the dog walk by a person who is very close, such as 1 foot (30.5cm) away. Have the dog circle this person.
- Add a second person to your "crowd." You can have your dog walk by two people who are milling around from 5 feet (1.5m) away, then 3 feet (0.9m) away, and so on.
- Add the third person to your crowd.
- Now have your crowd help you by moving toward your dog as they would if they were walking down a sidewalk on a busy street. Go several feet, turn around, and repeat.
- After your dog has mastered walking around a small number of people in training sessions and in the real world, you can begin to add experiences that involve a greater number of people, such as walking on a busy sidewalk, taking your dog to a dog show, or attending a community event.

Getting Started with People Weaves

To prepare dogs to walk close to people in a class situation, students in a CGC class can help one another. Begin with the students in a line, with about 6 feet (1.8m) between each person. With his or her dog on leash, the handler at the end of the line begins weaving in and out of the line of students.

The next task is to have the students in a circle with enough space between them for a person and dog to pass through. The handler and dog weave in and out of the circle of students. In an advanced class, for dogs that have no trouble weaving in and out of the line and circle of people, the students who are helping can have their own (well-controlled) dogs on leash, sitting at their sides, as the handler and dog do the exercises.

Unusual Crowds

By now, your dog is able to walk close to several people with no problems. It is time to add things to your practice sessions that your dog has never seen. Consider adding someone wearing a raincoat or hat to the crowd. A crowd member can walk along with a shopping bag or purse. If you are a female who lives alone, and your dog has few opportunities to interact with men, you should practice with men in the crowd. If you live in a neighborhood with children, you should also provide opportunities for your dog to get to know children during training. Make sure that the dog is under good control before approaching children, and be sure to obtain the permission of the children's parents.

Skills for Therapy Dogs

The Canine Good Citizen Program is a great place to start if you aspire to have your dog registered or certified as a therapy dog. Many therapy dog organizations require that dogs pass the CGC Test as a prerequisite to their own therapy specific screenings.

If you will be volunteering with your dog, you'll find out that therapy dogs need to be able to walk through a crowd. The crowd could be in the hallway of a school for special-needs children or in the dayroom of an assisted-living facility. People in the crowd in a therapeutic setting may be using equipment such as walkers, canes, wheelchairs, IV poles, crutches, and electric carts. Incorporating healthcare equipment into practice sessions is essential for a dog that will be taking a therapy dog test and working in a special setting.

If you have a shy dog that loves people but is afraid of healthcare equipment, such as wheelchairs, you may need a special training program to desensitize your dog to the equipment. Remember that desensitization involves taking small, slow steps toward the desired behavior. To accustom a dog to a wheelchair, you would begin with the wheelchair on the opposite side of the room. Bring the dog into the room and praise him for calm behavior. Next, move a few steps closer to the wheelchair. Praise the dog. Repeat this process until you are next to the wheelchair.

Next, have a volunteer sit in the chair and talk to the dog. The helper can offer the dog a treat. Finally, when the dog is calm around the chair, the helper can begin to slowly move the chair.

Hiding Behind the Handler

Dogs that attempt to hide behind their handlers during the Walking through a Crowd exercise are most often dogs that need more socialization to feel comfortable around people. These may be dogs whose owners work all day, exercise their dogs mainly in the backyard, and don't really get around to introducing their dogs to new people. Or these may be rescue or shelter dogs that had rough starts in life. Their owners should be applauded for giving these dogs another chance.

If your goal is to eventually have your dog participate in therapy work, healthcare equipment, such as walkers and crutches, should be used when training for Test Item 5.

To work with a dog that is afraid of people in a crowd, remember to break the task into smaller parts using shaping. Start with introducing your dog to one new person. The helper can begin by sitting on the floor and allowing the dog to approach. Eventually, the helper should stand up and begin to move around. Your helper can give the dog a treat so that the dog learns that good things can come from people. After the dog is working well with a single person, introduce the dog to a second new person, and, eventually, invite more than one person at a time to meet your dog.

Expanding Your Dog's World

Item 5 of the Canine Good Citizen Test ensures that a dog can move with his handler while in public places that may be crowded and busy with people. Teaching your dog to walk through a crowd and perfecting this skill will expand your dog's world by increasing the chances that he'll be invited to tag along when you go places. Sharing experiences with your canine best friend will strengthen the bond and enhance the wonderful life you have together.

SIT AND DOWN ON COMMAND/ STAYING IN PLACE

This test demonstrates that the dog has training and will respond to the handler's commands to sit and down and will remain in the place demonstrated by the handler. The dog must (1) sit on cue and (2) down on cue, then (3) stay in a sit or down. Note that in the CGC Test, the dog demonstrates that he will do both sit and down.

So, it looks like this: "Show me your dog can sit on cue. Great! Now show me your dog will go down on cue. Great! Now it's time for the stay—you choose the position, sit or down, leave your dog, and walk out to the end of this line."

Prior to this test, the dog's leash is removed and replaced with a 20-foot (6m) line (or a 15-foot [4.5m] line is attached to the dog's leash). The handler may take a reasonable amount of time and use more than one command to make the dog sit and then down. The Evaluator must determine if the dog has responded to the handler's commands. The handler may not use excessive force to put the dog into either position, but he or she may touch the dog to offer gentle guidance.

When instructed by the Evaluator, the handler tells the dog to stay and walks to the end of the 20-foot (6m) line, turns, and returns immediately to the dog at a normal pace. The dog must remain in the place he was left (he may change position, such as standing up).

- The 20-foot (6m) line is used for safety. If the CGC Test is indoors in a secure area, the Evaluator may choose to have the dog drag the leash or work off leash in this exercise. Any time the test is given in an outdoor area, the Evaluator should keep the safety of the dog foremost in mind.
- There are no breed-specific exceptions for sitting.
- Pulling the dog's front legs out from a sit position (so the dog automatically drops into a down) is beyond gentle guidance, and the dog should not pass the test.

CGC Test Item 6 builds skills that can be used to manage your dog's behavior.

- To prevent a beginning handler from tugging on the long line as he or she leaves the dogs (and thus pulling the dog out of the stay) an Evaluator can do the following: (1) lay the 20-foot (6m) line stretched out on the floor, (2) instruct the handler to attach the line to the dog's collar, (3) give the handle end of the line to the handler after the line is attached, and (4) instruct the handler to walk to the end of the line (while holding on to the end).
- The dog is left for the stay in a sit or down. As the handler returns, if the dog simply stands but does not leave the place where the handler left him, the dog passes the test. A dog that walks forward to the handler should not pass.
- Dogs that do not sit or down after a reasonable period of time need more training and should not pass.
- The handler should not go to the end of the line and call the dog; he or she should return to the dog.

Special Sit Considerations

In CGC Test Item 2, Sitting Politely for Petting, we explained how to teach the dog to sit. We also described the two primary uses of the sit, which are (1) as a skill in daily activities, such as sitting to get a treat, and (2) as a behavior-control technique. In particular, sit can be used as a DRI procedure when sitting is incompatible with a problem behavior (such as jumping up on guests).

There are two additional topics related to teaching sit and the CGC Program. The first topic deals with breed-specific exceptions to the sit in the CGC Test. There are no breed-specific exceptions—all dogs must pass all ten test items to pass the CGC Test. The second topic relates to dogs that are being shown in AKC conformation shows and whether teaching the sit in CGC training will affect a show dog's performance in the ring. Should conformation dogs be taught to sit on command?

Conformation is the event in which the physical structure of a dog is evaluated by a licensed judge. The dog begins in the standing position, and, when the handler is instructed by the judge, the handler moves the dog around the ring so the judge can observe the dog's movement and gait. After moving, the dog returns to the standing position in the lineup of dogs so that any time the judge looks at the whole lineup, he or she can evaluate all of the dogs at once. In conformation, judges assess dogs on areas that include physical structure, general appearance, condition of coat, gait/ movement, and temperament.

For the Stay in Place Test, the handler may choose to leave the dog in a sit or down position.

Just as there are no breed-specific exceptions to CGC Test Items, there are no exceptions made for dogs whose owners believe that the time is not quite right to teach all of the skills. If the time is not right for your dog to learn all of the CGC skills, we suggest waiting to try to earn the CGC award until you can train him for all of the ten required skills.

However, with some behavioral know-how, there is no reason why a conformation dog can't be taught to sit for the CGC Test. The behavioral principle that comes into play here is called *stimulus control* (or *stimulus discrimination*, which is the process for teaching stimulus control). Examples of stimulus control in the real world include the following:

- The child who has learned that yelling on the playground is fine but that it is not acceptable to scream in a library.
- The driver who knows she can fail to stop at a stop sign if no one is around but realizes that running the stop sign is never a good idea, especially if there is a car nearby that has blue and red lights on top.
- The high-school student who has learned which teachers will allow him to get away with sleeping in study hall and which ones will report him to the principal for snoring instead of studying.

Dogs are keenly intelligent, amazing creatures that can easily be taught to know what is expected of them in different situations. One trick for teaching dogs to discriminate between an activity that requires standing and one that allows sitting is to use different collars for different activities. For example, a fine, light show lead signals to the dog that it is time for the conformation ring, whereas a thicker buckle collar signals that you're getting ready to do obedience.

A second trick for ensuring that your dog will know what is expected of him is to teach the words (verbal cues) that are relevant to each activity. In preparation for the CGC Test, a dog learns verbal cues such as sit, down, and come. A conformation dog can be taught the word "stand," and the conformation handler can give the dog the verbal reminder to stand as soon as there is any sign that the dog is beginning to sit. With a few reminders paired with food rewards for standing, any attempts at sitting in the conformation ring will soon disappear.

Teaching Down on Command

Knowing how to lie down on cue is another basic must-have skill for all dogs. Like the sit command, down can be used in practical settings when you need your dog to take a break, and it can also be used as a behavior-control technique.

In CGC Test Item 6, the dog demonstrates correct responses to the handler's verbal cues.

For many dogs, down is harder to learn than sit. The good news is that the down is an easier position for most dogs to maintain than the sit. The dog can become more relaxed (even to the point of falling asleep) in the down position, and many dogs are more likely to stay in the down position during competitive events. When you need your dog to stay in position for a longer period of time (such as while you eat a meal), it's more humane for you to ask him to lie down than to sit, because he will be more comfortable.

DOGS WITH DISABILITIES

Dogs with disabilities are the only dogs for which exceptions are made in the CGC Test. Dogs that use carts because they don't have use of their back legs may not be able to sit or lie down. These dogs are welcome in the test, and accommodations are made so that they can participate.

Steps to Teaching Down

There are several methods for teaching down on command. The main consideration is to choose a method that is not traumatic for the dog, which means that you should absolutely avoid using force—no pushing or pulling the dog into position. Using force will do nothing to enhance your relationship with your dog, and pushing hard on the dog's hips can cause physical damage.

In a CGC training class, dogs and owners practice together, which helps the dogs get used to distractions.

1. First, get ready. As you've done when teaching other skills, choose a time when you have about twenty minutes, uninterrupted, that you can devote to a training session. You can do this lesson indoors, in which case you don't need to have the dog on leash unless you need the leash for control (e.g., in case the dog says "See you later!"). If you are training outdoors in a public place, keep your dog on leash.

2. Get your treat bag or put a few pieces of your dog's favorite food in your pocket.

3. Maintain a good attitude. For canines, down can be a position of submission. When you first begin training, a strong-willed dog may not be eager to lie down and may resist. You'll have to balance being consistent and firm with making the training session seem like fun. Make sure you have identified a reinforcer (reward) that the dog wants.

4. Begin with your dog in a sit at your left side. You can give the dog a taste of the treat when you begin so he'll know what is coming. Then, hold the treat in front of the dog's nose. The treat should be close to his nose (about 1 to 2 inches [2.5 to 5cm] away).

5. As you say "Down," move the treat in a straight line down to the ground, right in front of the dog's front feet. Keep your palm down and your hand closed. The speed with which you move the food to the floor will depend on the speed of your dog. You can experiment with this. With a fast-moving, energetic dog (think of a wound-up Labrador Retriever), you may be able to move your hand a little faster. With a slower-moving dog (think of a Basset Hound), moving more slowly may help the dog focus on the food.

   With a small dog, you may want to put the dog on a table for training so that you don't have to bend over. If you decide to use a table, make sure it has a nonslip surface. Or, if you are in good physical shape, you can get on your knees to work with a smaller dog. With a larger dog, you'll have to bend over to move the food

If you're going to train with food, you can give the dog a taste of the treat to start so he will know what is coming and will be motivated to get it.

in your hand to the floor. Remember to use good body mechanics and bend your knees rather than bending forward with a rounded back, or you may find yourself with a back problem.

6. As soon as you say "Down" and lower the food, most dogs will start to drop into the down position to follow the food. If your dog doesn't go all the way down, move the food out, away from the dog. This will get the dog into the down position.

7. Timing is everything. As soon as the dog is in the correct position, praise him ("Good dog, down!") and, at the same time, give him the food reward. Remember to praise and give the food immediately as soon as the dog is in the down position.

8. End on a high note. Have the dog get up. Put the dog in a sit and repeat the previous steps a few times. After a few successful responses, end the training session and have some fun playtime together.

9. Phase out the food. As your dog gets more proficient with the down on command, things will happen faster, and you'll be able to eliminate the food lure and simply use your empty hand to signal the dog to lie down. Hand signals are permitted in the CGC Test. Eventually, your dog will respond to only the verbal cue without food or a hand signal.

10. Change your position. As your dog learns the down on command exercise, practice moving around and giving the cue from the side of the dog, from the front of the dog, and from a distance.

Some dogs can relax completely in the down position.

Choose Your Words Wisely

A final word about teaching the down on command. When you are teaching the dog to lie down, you are most likely to use the verbal cue "Down." This means that the dog will pair the word down with dropping into the down position. If you have a dog that jumps up, choose a different word (other than "Down") to indicate that the dog should stop jumping on people, your priceless antique sofa, or whatever else he is jumping on. Use a word such as "Off" when your dog jumps up; restrict the use of the word "Down" to when you want him to lie down. This will eliminate confusion for the dog.

Teaching Staying in Place

Combined with a reliable sit and down, having the dog stay in place is another powerful tool when it comes to sharing a peaceful life with your dog. We want you to spend plenty of time training, exercising, playing with, and loving your dog, but there are times when dogs need to lie down and stay there.

DID YOU KNOW?

Keep in mind that shy dogs and dogs that are extremely fearful (particularly shelter or rescue dogs that may have been abused) might resist lying down because they have not learned to trust people and thus will not want to assume a vulnerable position. As a part of the whole training package, these dogs will need a lot of confidence-building activities and a rich schedule of reinforcement.

The stay command is important for keeping your dog safe and out of trouble. A reliable stay can be used when you want your dog to wait before crossing the street, when he needs to stay in position for a veterinary check, when you and your dog are around a child who is afraid of dogs, or when you want your dog to stay while you receive a delivery or talk to the postal worker. A reliable stay actually gives the dog far more freedom because once you have this skill perfected, you'll find that you can take your dog to many more places.

While hand signals are permitted in the CGC Test, ideally your goal will be to teach your dog to respond to verbal cues without accompanying hand signals.

You can teach your dog to stay in the sit, stand, or down position. For the CGC Test, you will choose sit or down and then leave the dog, walk out 20 feet (6m), and immediately return. If you go beyond CGC to AKC obedience training, the dog will be required at the Novice level to do a one-minute sit-stay and a three-minute down-stay. It's a good idea to teach both a sit-stay and down-stay from the beginning. You can also work on stand-stay because this skill has many practical uses, such as when the dog needs to be groomed or visit the veterinarian.

Sit-Stay

1. Be prepared. Have your food rewards ready. If you are outdoors in a park or other location without secure fencing, keep the dog on a leash. Otherwise, you can teach stay without the leash, although you might need it if your dog decides to go AWOL in the middle of a training session.
2. Start with your dog sitting beside you on your left side. Put out your left hand, with the palm facing the dog's face, about 6 to 12 inches (15 to 30cm) from the dog's nose and say "Stay." Make sure that your dog can see your hand signal. This is an easy step, as the dog was already sitting and staying. Reinforce the stay with praise, such as "Good stay."

Note: Some instructors will teach you to use your left hand for the stay signal; others prefer the right hand. In the method described here, we suggest that you use your left hand so that you don't have to reach across your body with your right hand. Further, if you are working with the dog on a leash, it is likely you will be holding the leash in your right hand, so using your left hand to signal the stay will be easier.

3. With the dog still sitting at your side, give the hand signal as you say "Stay." This time, you are going to pivot to stand right in front of the dog. To pivot, you'll lift your right foot and swing it around so it is in front of the dog, then bring your left foot next to your right foot. Say "Good stay."

4. Reverse the procedure to pivot back so that you're beside the dog again. Move your left foot back into position beside the dog, then swing your right foot around to be beside your left foot. Praise the dog and give him a treat for staying.

5. Next, you are going begin working on gradually and slowly increasing your distance away from the dog while he remains in a stay. Say "Stay" and pivot to again position yourself in front of the dog. Then take one step back so that you're about 18 inches (46cm) away from the dog. Stay in this position for about five seconds. Reinforce the dog for staying with praise and a treat.

6. Continue this process, each time moving back a little farther—two steps, four steps, and so on. Return to the dog each time. At this point in training, do not call the dog to come to you after you have instructed him to stay. This is confusing and will result in a dog that predicts you'll always ask for a recall (coming to you) after the stay. You'll end up with a dog that breaks the stay position in order to get to you.

7. If you are using a leash, you'll eventually be beyond the length of the 6-foot (1.8m) leash. If you are working outside, you can use a long line to ensure that your dog does not run away.

Once your dog has mastered a solid, reliable stay, this is a behavior that can keep your dog safe.

Down-Stay

The down-stay is very much like the sit-stay. To give the stay hand signal, you'll have to bend over for larger and medium-sized dogs, and you'll have to bend way over for small dogs. With the dog in a down, repeat the steps in the sit-stay exercise. Once the dog is in position, the owner gives the stay hand signal before walking away from the dog.

Increasing Distances When Teaching Stay

When a dog is not successful at learning to stay on command, chances are there is an overzealous owner at the other end of the leash. Distances of 10, 15, and 20 feet (3, 4.5, and 6m) don't sound so far to the average human, so a beginning trainer might take a beginning dog, say "Stay" for the very first time, and instantly move 20 feet (6m) away from the dog. This is in the category of "too far too fast."

Remember that teaching every new skill should begin with very small steps so the dog can be successful. In teaching stay, you should very gradually lengthen your distance away from the dog and the length of time you expect the dog to remain in a sit-stay or down-stay.

In the Staying in Place part of Test Item 6, you will leave your dog in a stay, walk out 20 feet (6m), turn around, and immediately return to the dog.

THE 20-FOOT LINE

In the CGC Test, if the test is outdoors, the Evaluator will ask you to attach a 20-foot (6m) line to your dog's collar. You may want to practice this before the actual test. The main things to remember when using the 20-foot (6m) line are (1) don't reel your dog in or out and (2) don't do anything to tug on the line. If you don't take care when handling the 20-foot (6m) line, you can pull a dog that is just beginning training out of the sit and cause him to not pass the CGC Test. In situations where there is adequate supervision, an Evaluator may decide to leave the line lying on the ground rather than have you try to manage the line.

Using a 20-foot (6m) line means letting it drape on the ground with slack between you and the dog.

The stay exercise in the CGC Test builds the foundation for more advanced stays, such as those done for longer periods of time.

Advanced Exercises

Once the dog knows sit, down, and stay, you can practice so that he's rock-solid when it comes to stay. Set up situations so the dog has to stay in the presence of distractors such as family members walking by, children at a park, someone playing ball (especially if the dog is ball-crazy), and people who are eating.

If the dog breaks the stay, meaning he gets up before you release him (by saying something such as "OK, let's go!"), don't respond with emotion. Quietly go to the dog and take him back to where he was supposed to stay. Put the dog in a stay and walk away. Praise the dog when he stays.

If you continue training classes beyond CGC, there are many exercises in which you'll practice the stay. Here are some stay exercises done in classes:

❊ The handlers, with their dogs on leashes, form a large circle. Following the instructor's directions, the handlers tell their dogs to stay and then leave their dogs and circle all the way around the ring. When the handlers return to their own dogs, they praise if the dogs have stayed in place.

❊ The handlers, with their dogs on leashes, get in a long line, side by side, with about 5 feet (1.5m) between each dog-and-handler team. One handler, with his dog on leash, begins at one end of the line and weaves in and out of the other handlers and their dogs. A very advanced version of this exercise is to have the lined-up handlers put their dogs in down-stays and then leave their dogs. The handler/dog team then weaves in and out of the line of dogs. An experienced instructor can decide when a training class is ready to try this.

Your instructor may teach some stay exercises that are similar to the beginning exercises in competition obedience. One exercise will require your dog to stand-stay (called the Stand for Exam) for a brief examination by a judge. You will stand your dog and step away, and the judge will walk up to the dog and lightly touch the dog's head, body, and hindquarters. Another more advanced stay exercise will require the dog to do a one-minute sit-stay. You will tell your dog to sit, then go to stand on the opposite side of the ring until your instructor tells you to return. After the sit-stay, the exercise can be done with a down-stay.

CGC Test Item 7

COMING WHEN CALLED

This test demonstrates that the dog will come when called by the handler. With the dog still on the 20-foot (6m) line from Test Item 6, the handler will walk 10 feet (3m) from the dog, turn to face the dog, and call the dog. The handler may use body language and encouragement when calling the dog.

The handler may give a verbal cue such as "Stay" or "Wait" (or something similar) or may simply walk away. The handler may leave the dog in the sit, down, or standing position. If the dog attempts to follow the handler, the Evaluator may distract the dog (e.g., with petting) until the handler is 10 feet (3m) away. The test is complete when the dog comes to the handler and the handler attaches the dog's own leash. This exercise does not test the stay; this exercise tests whether the dog will come when called.

- Dogs that attempt to follow their handlers should not be failed. In such a case, the Evaluator should distract the dog. The test begins when the handler calls the dog.
- The handler can bend down to call the dog, pat his or her legs, and make encouraging sounds.
- Handlers may call the dog more than once (two or three attempts), but the dog should not be passed if many repeated prompts are required.
- A dog should not be passed if the handler uses the long line to "reel in" the dog. The dog should come on his own when called. The Evaluator who sees that a handler is starting to reel the dog in may stop the exercise, give instructions to the handler, and start over.

In CGC Test Item 7, the dog is on a long line and is called by his owner from a distance of 10 feet (3m).

Adding Coming When Called to the CGC Test

Coming When Called, Item 7 of the Canine Good Citizen Test, is perhaps one of the most important skills an owner can teach a dog. This exercise can be used to save a dog's life or remove a dog from a potentially dangerous situation. Coming when called is also a practical skill that is needed many times each day when living with a dog. The dog is called to get his collar on to go for a walk. The dog is called into the kitchen to eat. The dog is called to come into the backyard or to come to his owner at a dog park. Coming when called is a necessary prerequisite for participation in so many activities, and a dog that reliably responds to the come command can have more freedom. The list of instances in which a dog should come when called is endless.

The Canine Good Citizen Test was adopted in 1989 and, in an early version of the test, Coming When Called was not included. The developers of the test believed that by the time a dog was ready to take the CGC Test, he would certainly be coming to his owner when called and, therefore, the item was not really needed on the test. These were the days before the Internet, when if you wanted to express your opinions about something, you had to locate the right person and his or her contact information, write a letter, address an envelope, and find a stamp. Yet despite the time and trouble it took to do this, in the first few years of the CGC Test, hundreds of people wrote to say that coming when called was one of the most important behaviors that a dog needed to learn and that the test was incomplete without it.

In 1994, the Coming When Called test item was added to the CGC Test. It replaced the Praise and Interaction exercise because, after a few years of observing the test in action, the AKC felt that it didn't make sense for owners to praise their dogs during only one of the test items. Praise should be given for all test items, and owners are encouraged to praise their dogs throughout the test.

Why Coming When Called Is Important

When an owner begins working with his or her puppy very early, bonding (that sometimes looks like imprinting) occurs, and the result is a puppy that will follow his owner and come when called from anywhere, at any time, on or off leash. For most dogs, however, teaching a reliable come (or recall) takes some work. Even with an owner who practices with the dog every day, has a good instructor, and keeps a log of progress, it can take a year to get the dog to the point that he will come when called in a large area like a field or park. But the work that goes into this level of training has a significant payoff that will last for the lifetime of the dog.

How to Teach Coming When Called

As with many of the other CGC skills, coming when called should be taught using the behavioral principle of *shaping*. In shaping this skill, you'll begin by teaching your dog to come to you from very short distances. Over time, you'll gradually lengthen the distance. In the initial stages of training, your dog may come from only a few feet (about a meter) away. For the CGC Test, your dog will be required to come when called from 10 feet (3m) away. Hopefully, you'll continue your training, and your dog will ultimately respond to "Come" from across a field.

Another part of the shaping involved in teaching your dog to come when called involves the introduction of distractions. In the beginning, your training will be done in quiet sessions with few distractions. As training progresses, you should add distractions, such as other people moving around as you call your dog, someone playing with a ball, birds flying as you practice in a field (a big distraction for sporting breeds), and other dogs moving around.

Method 1: Kneel Down to Call the Dog

One method for teaching a dog to come is to make yourself seem very interesting by kneeling down, opening your arms or clapping, using a very happy and enthusiastic voice, and calling your dog. When the dog gets to you, you should praise him and give him a treat. This method is particularly suitable for puppies in the early stages of training.

In the CGC Test, it is acceptable for owners to clap their hands, bend over, and otherwise encourage their dogs to come when called.

Only practice the come exercise off leash when indoors or in another secure area.

Method 2: Teaching Coming When Called When Out for a Walk

You've been working on having your dog walk on a loose leash and, hopefully, you have been going on some nice walks with your dog. Now it's time to add the Coming When Called exercise. Get your dog and leash and start walking.

1. Walk along with the dog on your left side. When the dog is not quite expecting it, quickly begin backing up, saying, "Come!" When the dog comes to you, praise him and give him a treat.
2. To make the exercise seem more like a game and to build a quick recall, walk along with the dog on leash. When he is not expecting it, run backward several steps, saying, "Come!" Give him a treat and praise for coming.

Method 3: Teaching Coming When Called from the Sit-Stay

1. Put your dog in a sit-stay at your left side. The dog's leash should be attached to his collar.
2. Tell your dog to stay (or wait, whatever command you use to tell the dog to stay in position).
3. As you did when teaching the stay, pivot so that you are standing in front of your dog.
4. Step back one step. Say "Come," calling your dog. If the dog does not move, give a little tug on the leash to have him come to you. When the dog comes to you, praise and give him a treat. If your dog comes to you in slow motion, as though he is not eager

By kneeling down, you encourage the dog to come to you.

If you decide to compete in obedience, you should polish your recall skills so that you can stand up straight and call your dog to "sit front," as shown here.

to do this, run backward a few steps, enthusiastically calling him to come. Most often, when you move faster, the dog will respond and begin to trot to get to you.

5. Walk in a small circle with the dog and set him up again in a sit-stay.

6. This time, go to the end of your 6-foot (1.8m) leash to call the dog. Call him, then praise him when he comes to you.

7. Mix it up—don't be predictable. If every time you leave your dog in a stay, you go out some distance and then call him to come, he will learn that he is always going to come to you after being told to stay. In obedience competitions, dogs are often disqualified for breaking the stay to come to their handlers. They are victims of this training mistake. To prevent this problem, even when you are training your dog to come when called, you should sometimes tell the dog to stay and then return to the dog without calling him to come. Reinforce the dog for staying.

8. Phase out the food. Remember, if you choose to use food, it is a good initial reinforcer for teaching a new skill, but the ultimate goal is for your dog to want to come to you when you call him. After he has learned to come when called, start phasing out the food rewards to an intermittent schedule (so the dog will get plenty of praise but will only get food every now and then; this is called a *variable schedule of reinforcement*).

9. Add a new behavior to the chain: the sit in front. Your dog has already learned to sit. As you work on coming when called, begin to have your dog come and then sit in front of you before you reinforce (reward) him. This is an example of the behavioral process called *chaining*, in which you combine behaviors in a planned sequence. If you decide to compete in formal obedience, your dog will need to come to you, sit in front of you, and then "finish" by returning to the sitting position at your left side.

Method 4: Coming When Called on a Long Line

This method is really a variation of Method 3, with the main difference being that you will work with a long line or retractable leash to teach the dog to come when called from a longer distance, such as 20 feet (6m). A retractable leash has a mechanism in the handle that allows the line to be extended or to roll up inside the handle. The handler can push a button to lock the leash so that no more line can be released or so that the length of line already released does not automatically retract. The idea is much like a fishing line that can be reeled in and out.

1. Choose the equipment that you will use. A long line is inexpensive and may be easier to use than a retractable leash. The disadvantage is that the line can get tangled. Retractable leashes do not easily tangle; however, if you are clumsy in handling the leash, you can pull the dog out of a sit-stay.

2. Put the dog at your left side. Tell the dog to stay (or wait), walk out to the end of the line, wait a few seconds, and then call the dog to come. What you don't want

Practicing this exercise on a long line mirrors what you will do in the CGC Test.

to do is walk to the end of the long line and immediately call the dog every single time. The dog will quickly learn that as soon as you get out 20 feet (6m), he will be called to come, so he'll start anticipating the recall and will come before he is called. Vary the length of time that you wait before calling the dog. And remember, sometimes you are going to walk to the end of the line and return to the dog without calling him. Varying the length of time that the dog needs to wait along with varying the recalls will teach your dog to pay attention to you.

3. As you did with the shorter leash, you'll use shaping with the long line. Start with having the dog come 5, then 10, then 20 feet (1.5, then 3, then 6m). If the dog is moving slowly when coming to you, run backward, excitedly calling him to you. You can also clap your hands.

4. Give a small tug on the leash if the dog stays in the sit-stay and does not come to you when called.

5. When your dog comes when called, don't forget the praise (and treats if you are training with food rewards).

6. Work to phase out food rewards, eventually offering them on an intermittent schedule. *You* should be the reward.

7. If you are using a hand signal to get the dog to come, you'll start by pairing the hand signal with the verbal cue "Come." Eventually, if you compete in obedience at the advanced levels, you will stop using the verbal cue and will use a hand signal only.

When an Off-Leash Dog Won't Come

Have you ever been to a park or hiking area and seen an off-leash dog running across a field with an out-of-breath, frustrated owner following far behind, screaming at the dog to come back? What's gone wrong here? There are numerous reasons why a dog that is moving faster than a speeding bullet across an open area has gone "selectively deaf" and chosen to ignore his owner's pleas to come.

To help you troubleshoot any problems you might be having related to your dog's not coming when called, here are the most common issues.

- The dog is not ready to be off leash in a large, open outdoor space and needs more systematic training on recalls. Go back to the basics and move forward from there.

- There may be competing reinforcers. Perhaps you have a trained dog that is usually happy to come to you when called, but if you have a sporting dog in a field where there are birds, or a sighthound in the woods where there are rabbits, you may have lost the competition for your dog's attention. It is important to know your dog well. This means that you know when it is safe to take the leash off and, more importantly, when it is a good idea to leave the leash on.

- Sometimes the dog won't come to you because you have not established yourself as a reinforcer. Sorry to hurt your feelings, but the dog would say you're no fun!

- At home, if the only times you call the dog to you are to clip his nails, clean his teeth, and do other things that the dog doesn't enjoy, he may be reluctant to come to you when called.

- You may not have established a history of positive reinforcement for coming when called. Here's an example: You're at the dog park. You call the dog. He comes to you. You don't say anything to him, you put on his leash, and you put him in the car to leave the park. It's no surprise that the dog is not too excited about coming to you the next time you call him!

- You may not understand the dog's needs. Sometimes a dog won't come when called because you have not allowed his basic needs to be met—the dog may need to run off some energy, sniff around to gather information, or search a little longer for a good place for a bathroom break.

What to Do if the Dog Won't Come When Called

What about a dog that won't come when you call? When you've fed, walked, played with, cleaned up after, and done everything else a good owner should do for his or her dog, there's a good chance you'll be embarrassed, frustrated, or angry if the dog completely ignores you. No matter how you feel, it is important that you don't get emotional. *Never, ever* call a dog and punish him when he comes to you. This will destroy your relationship with your dog and will ensure that he will never do well at coming when called.

If you are in a park or open field where off-leash exercise is permitted and the dog won't come to you, do not chase him. Chasing causes animals (dogs included) to run away from you. Instead, in the emergency situation where your dog is moving away from you, look like you're having plenty of fun where you are. Make a high-pitched, interesting noise as you move away from the dog. There is a good chance that he'll come to see what is going on, and then you can praise and reward him for coming to you. Once you've got your dog back and know that he is safe, you can put the leash on him and do some training on coming when called. If you are in a situation where there are just too many temptations for the dog (such as other off-leash dogs), you may need to keep your dog on leash for the remainder of the time. You can go back to off-leash training in safe, controlled places such as your house, a fenced yard, or a training class.

A 20-foot (6m) long line is used in the Coming When Called Test Item.

REACTION TO ANOTHER DOG

This test demonstrates that the dog can behave politely around other dogs. Two handlers and their dogs approach each other from a distance of about 15 feet (4.5m), stop, exchange pleasantries, and continue on.

- The dog should show no more than a casual interest in the distraction dog. If the dog attempts to go to or jump on the distraction dog, he should not pass the test.
- The dog may move slightly toward the other dog/handler, then stop. The dog must stay back from the other dog/handler.
- The dog can stretch his neck and sniff without moving forward to the other dog/handler.
- When the handlers stop to exchange pleasantries, the dog does not have to sit. He can remain standing beside the handler. If the dog remains standing, he should not cross over in front of the handler to go to the other dog.
- The conversation between handlers can be brief: "Hi, good to see you again. Give me a call sometime."
- As the handler leaves, if the dog turns around and begins pulling as if to follow the other dog/handler, the dog should not pass the test.
- If the distraction dog causes a disruption, the dog can be tested again with a more appropriate distraction dog. The distraction dog should have been observed or evaluated before the test to ensure that he is reliable.

CGC Test Item 8, Reaction to Another Dog, in which two dogs are required to politely walk past each other, is a necessary skill for walks in the community, therapy dog work, visits to dog parks, and being anywhere in the presence of other dogs. Dogs that are boarded while their owners go on vacation need to have acceptable reactions to other dogs, as do any dogs participating in organized dog events such as training classes, dog shows, and "meet-ups." Sometimes, dogs don't have good reactions to other dogs, and this is a problem that should be addressed by the owners.

Canine Good Citizen training results in dogs that react appropriately to other dogs.

Lunging

When a dog lunges at another dog while both are walking along on leash, the lunging is often interpreted as a sign of dog-to-dog aggression, but this isn't always the case. Behavior analysts, both those for humans and those for dogs, are professionals who study behavior. They work to understand the meaning of individual behaviors by conducting functional assessments.

For example, consider the case of a crying human infants. It would be a mistake to assume that every infant was crying for the same reason and to address each problem in the same manner, such as by offering a pacifier to every crying baby. Babies cry for any number of reasons, and when an infant cries, a parent soon learns to run through the checklist—is the baby hungry, tired, wet, cold, or thirsty? If the baby is crying because he is cold, he needs a blanket, not a pacifier. If the baby is crying because he is wet, he needs a clean diaper, not a pacifier. Depending on the cause of the baby's crying, the solutions will vary.

Dogs are no different. There are different functions for their behaviors. Understanding that there are different functions for behaviors will help dog owners know better how to address problems.

In CGC Test Item 8, two handlers will approach from 15 feet (4.5m), exchange pleasantries, and continue on. Their dogs may show casual interest in each other but no signs of aggression.

Common Causes of On-Leash Lunging

- Dog-to-dog aggression. While some dogs are truly dog-aggressive, this is not usually the cause of lunging. If your dog plays well with other dogs in the dog park or during doggy playdates in your yard, chances are, if he lunges when on a leash, the cause of the behavior is not dog-aggression but is one of the other causes listed here.
- Fear. Dogs that are afraid of other dogs will sometimes lunge and bark when on leash. This is often the case with small dogs that put on loud, disruptive displays in the form of raucous barking. These are dogs that, through their barking and lunging on the leash, are saying, "I'm afraid. If I make a lot of noise and jump at you, you will be scared and will not try to hurt me."
- Protection of their owners. Some dogs are protective and take exception to anyone or any other dog coming near their owners. Such a dog will bark and make an assertive attempt to get between his owner and the approaching dog. This is often seen when a dog lives with only one person in the household, and this person may have unintentionally reinforced protective behaviors.
- Desire to play. Some dogs that bark and pull on their leashes may look scary, but they are simply barking out of excitement. These are dogs that desperately want to play. Particularly when dogs are larger and have the accompanying louder, deeper barks of larger dogs, the canine-communication version of "Let's play! Let's play! Chase me! Chase me!" is sometimes mistakenly interpreted as a precursor to aggression. Once they get excited and wound up, these dogs

can be challenging to manage if they have had no training and do not respond to instructions. Such dogs may have been properly socialized by their owners but have not been trained in basic good-behavior skills. Teaching dogs to walk nicely on a leash (CGC Test Item 4) and using the verbal cues "Let's walk" or "Heel" are some of the tricks to managing this problem.

🐾 Lack of socialization. For many species, including humans, other primates such as chimpanzees, and dogs, there is a critical period of socialization when young. If dogs are not exposed to new experiences, people, and other dogs during that time, they can have difficulties responding appropriately to other dogs. Unsocialized dogs don't know how to act around other dogs, so they engage in behaviors such as pulling on the leash, barking, or lunging. These dogs lack basic manners and canine social graces because they have not been exposed to other dogs and are uncertain about how they should approach and interact with members of their own species.

Neutering to Stop Lunging

Sometimes neutering is suggested as the solution for dogs that lunge aggressively at other dogs when on leash. Spaying and neutering have benefits, but it is important to understand that neutering is not a magic cure for behavior problems. Some people believe that behavior problems are testosterone-related and that simply neutering a dog will be an immediate fix. If your dog has a long-existing behavior problem with an established history of reinforcement, neutering the dog and doing nothing else will not solve the problem. If only it were that easy.

Training is the solution, and depending on the severity of the dog's behavior, you may need help from an instructor who is knowledgeable about canine behavior problems. A class designed to prepare you and your dog to take the Canine Good Citizen Test is a great place to teach your dog to react appropriately to another dog so that problems won't arise in the first place.

Earning the CGC award is an achievement that dog owners can be proud of.

Exercises to Teach CGC Test Item 8

1. Walking on a loose leash. First, make sure you have successfully taught your dog to walk on a leash (CGC Test Item 4, Walking on a Loose Leash) without another dog present.

2. Walking behind another dog. With your dog on a leash, walk about 20 feet (6m) behind another handler and dog. Can your dog do this? If so, try 10 feet (3m). Walking behind another dog is a good exercise for a dog that is shy and afraid of other dogs. If you attempt this exercise and your dog tries to drag you to the other dog, this may not be the exercise for you. Don't let the dog drag you; if he does, remember the exercise in which you turn and go in the opposite direction when your dog starts to pull.

3. Parallel walking. With your dog on a leash, walk parallel to another dog on a leash. The other dog should be 20 feet (6m) away, then 10 feet (3m), then 5 feet (1.5m). In parallel walking, you are walking side by side with another person and dog on a leash at the distances specified, and you are both going in the same direction. Can your dog do this? Walking parallel to another dog is less confrontational than walking toward another dog, as your dog will do in the CGC Test. If your dog begins to bark or lunge, widen the distance between the two dogs until your dog is comfortable. Gradually have the dogs walk closer to each other.

4. Walking toward another dog. Now it's time to have your dog walk toward another dog that is approaching; both dogs are on leash. Start about 20 feet (6m) apart, and you and the other handler will simply walk by each other, not stopping or saying anything. Can your dog do this? If so, gradually (in 3- to 5-foot [0.9- to 1.5m] increments, getting closer as your dog is successful at each new distance) close the gap so that you and the other handler get close enough to do a pretend handshake. When you can do this, your dog has learned the Reaction to Another Dog exercise of the CGC Test.

From the dog's perspective, walking behind another dog is much safer than approaching another dog and is less likely to trigger undesirable reactions such as barking, lunging, or fearful behavior.

Parallel walking is less threatening to a dog than approaching another dog head-on.

Shape your dog's appropriate reactions to another dog by starting at a distance and gradually getting closer.

What to Do if Your Dog Lunges

If your dog barks, lunges, or has any other trouble with any of the aforementioned exercises, remember shaping. Baby steps. Go back to the previous step or make the exercise easier. If your dog cannot tolerate walking beside a dog that is 5 feet (1.5m) away, go back to 10 feet (3m) and gradually decrease the distance. Remember to use plenty of praise and reinforcement (including food rewards) for successful responses. For most dogs, with a systematic approach and lots of reinforcement, it won't be long before passing other dogs on busy sidewalks and in class will not present a problem.

For a highly reactive dog that has had no socialization, you might need to do your training outside with a helper and another dog on leash to get enough space between the dogs. You might need to follow behind the other dog at a distance of 50 feet (15m) or more until your dog settles down.

For dogs that are having a hard time not lunging or barking excessively when another dog approaches on a leash, there are two other techniques that can be helpful.

1. Only move toward the other dog when your dog is behaving. When it comes time to approach another dog, if your dog jumps and lunges, turn around and go back in the opposite direction, away from the other dog. When your dog settles down, turn and approach the other dog again. You may need to repeat this multiple times, so choose one of your more patient friends to help you. This could take a while, so in the beginning you'll need to set aside time to make this a designated training session.

2. Use a "sit and watch" technique. By now, you've taught your dog a sit-stay. As soon as you see another dog approaching, move your dog some distance away and instruct him to sit. You can reinforce the dog for sitting. As soon as the other dog passes, you can go on your way, but do not allow your dog to drag you as if to chase after the other dog. When your dog can sit and watch another dog go by, you can graduate to having the dog stand and watch. Eventually, you'll be able to have your dog walking as the other dog approaches. Start a good distance away when you start doing "sit and watch" with your dog, and gradually get closer.

A SAFE DISTANCE

For safety, dogs remain on the outside of their handlers (on their handlers' left) during the CGC Test. They do not go nose to nose. When the dogs are close enough, the handlers should do a pretend handshake and exchange pleasantries (as specified in the CGC Test). Each handler should keep his dog's leash shortened enough so that the dog cannot pull across the handler and go to the other dog.

Socializing Adult Dogs

If your dog is having trouble with Reaction to Another Dog, don't get discouraged. If you have a dog that missed out on socializing with other dogs as a pup, you can develop an organized plan to help him win some canine friends. Try some of the aforementioned suggestions along with the following tips to develop a dog with world-class social skills.

- Start slowly. If your dog is nervous around other dogs, going to a dog park may be too much for his first step at getting acquainted, especially when there are twenty other dogs, including the canine schoolyard bully, racing around at top speed.
- Be systematic. Start by planning to meet one friend with only one dog at a designated time. Choose a dog that is well mannered and polite. If your dog is rowdy and dominant, and you are afraid that he might hurt another dog, have an experienced dog trainer with you during the initial interactions. Your dog can detect when you are nervous, and the presence of a confident, skilled observer will help you relax.
- Expose your dog to all types of dogs. If your purebred Papillon has only ever met others of his breed, he will get a real surprise the first time he encounters an Irish Wolfhound. Training classes provide you with an excellent place to expose your pup to small dogs, large dogs, quiet dogs, active dogs, dogs with long hair, dogs with short hair, and more.

Too-Social Dogs

Lunging is not the only problem seen in the Reaction to Another Dog exercise. Sometimes dogs just want to cross in front of their owners to get to another dog. They want to say hello, sniff, find out who the dog is, or initiate play. To pass the CGC Test, your dog will need to be trained well enough that this won't happen.

Basically, whether you are a dog or a person, getting along well with others and understanding the boundaries have a lot to do with experience and exposure. If you haven't done it already, attend an AKC dog show. You'll see many dogs of every breed that are standing within inches of each other, waiting to go into the ring. You'll see unflappable dogs of all shapes and sizes on leashes, being rushed past you through noisy, crowded areas. The handlers and owners of dogs shown in conformation have usually done an excellent job of socializing these dogs to other dogs, people, and loud noises. The dog show itself provides training opportunities that are endless.

WHY THE PRETEND HANDSHAKE?

We'll occasionally get a call from a person who says, "I don't shake hands with people I meet on the street. Why do you do this in the CGC Test?" When the CGC Test was developed, there was a long period of field testing. When observers would give handlers the instruction to pass by the other handler at a distance of about 3 feet (a little less than a meter), some would be at a distance of 3 feet, others would be closer, and still others would be as far as 6 feet (1.8m) from the other handler who was passing by with a dog on a leash. The handshake was implemented to help standardize the test. If handlers have to shake hands, they will be roughly the same distance apart when they stop in the Reaction to Another Dog exercise. In 2020, with concerns about COVID-19, the handshake was modified to a pretend handshake.

The handlers and dogs will eventually get close enough that the handlers can do a pretend handshake.

Generalization

Generalization is the behavioral term that refers to behaviors being seen in contexts other than those in which they were originally taught. For example, if you teach your dog to sit when a visitor comes to the front door, and the dog later sits when he meets someone in a park, we would say that the "sit for greeting" behavior has generalized across settings (however, with most dogs, this is not likely to happen without training). If you taught your dog to run and get his favorite stuffed animal when you come home, and he begins bringing the stuffed animal to visitors, we would say that the behavior of bringing the toy has *generalized* across people.

When a dog has a behavior problem, such as reacting inappropriately to another dog (by barking, lunging, or shying away), many people will tell you to take your dog

Using a "sit and watch" procedure will help a reactive dog learn to tolerate other dogs as they pass by.

to training classes. The idea is that your dog will have a chance to socialize with other dogs and will soon be ready to sail through CGC Test Item 8, Reaction to Another Dog, with flying colors.

In general, the suggestion to start attending classes when your dog has a behavior problem is excellent advice. In a class with a competent instructor, you'll learn to better communicate with your dog; your dog will be exposed to many new stimuli, including other dogs; and you'll learn new skills, such as sit, down, and stay, that can be used to manage behavior.

Here's what you need to watch out for, though. If you go to a group class where most of the dogs get along well with other dogs and the emphasis in the class is on other skills, such as teaching the dogs to heel, there's a good chance that your dog will not learn to interact appropriately with other dogs (or to perform Test Item 8). If you spend an hour each week in a circle, with the instructor saying, "Forward, halt. Forward, about turn, halt," your dog may be no better off at the end of the eight-week session when it comes to meeting another dog. You'll join the ranks of disappointed people who tell others, "I tried obedience training, and it didn't work."

Behaviorally, it is highly unlikely that generalization will occur across markedly different behaviors, such as the dog's learning to sit on cue and suddenly knowing how to react acceptably to an unfamiliar dog. A reliable sit-stay can keep your dog out of trouble when another dog approaches, but you also need actual practice with the specific Reaction to Another Dog Test Item.

If the class is not addressing your dog's problems, you might need to approach the instructor, talk about your specific issue, and ask to have some relevant exercises incorporated into the class. If this is not possible, ask if you can practice with other students and their dogs before the class begins.

At the Dog Park

Dog parks can be great places to provide opportunities for your dog to socialize with other canines, but there are a few things you should watch out for if you decide to take your dog to a dog park. One of the main concerns is that, unfortunately, some dog owners use the dog park as a break for themselves. Oblivious to what is going on, they sit and laugh and chat with other owners or bury their noses in books. Getting to know other dog owners who frequent a dog park is fine, as long as you supervise your own dog.

To make sure your dog is safe, keep an eye on the activity in the dog park. If you see a dog being overly rowdy with other dogs, ask the dog's owner if he can get his dog under control. Your four-legged friend will not learn a good lesson about socializing with other dogs if he spends his time at the dog park quivering under a bench while being intimidated by a larger dog.

Clothing on Dogs

The multi-billion-dollar pet industry is just one sign that people really love their dogs. Another sign is the rapidly increasing number of products for canines, including fancy dresses, boots, shoes, hats, coats, jewelry, and designer outfits. In places where there is cold and rainy weather, canine coats and boots can serve the very functional purpose of keeping dogs warm and dry. Other times, owners simply enjoy outfitting their dogs in canine clothes that range from everyday wear to expensive formalwear complete with pearls and diamonds.

For photo opportunities, special events (such as dog-o-ween), and the occasional indulgence of the owner, putting clothes a on dog for short periods of time probably doesn't hurt anything. But here are some things to remember about clothes on your pup:

- 🐾 Dogs are already wearing fur coats, and they can get easily overheated if you expect them to wear sailor suits or ruffled dresses when they are running around outside.
- 🐾 Dogs need to move around to sniff, explore, and make sense of their world. Some clothing for dogs can restrict movement or present safety risks by getting caught on objects.
- 🐾 Dogs are dogs; they are not babies or fashion accessories. We hope that if you put clothing on your dog, it's not a signal that you aren't letting the dog run through the grass, chase a bird off the fence, or do all of the other things dogs were bred to do.
- 🐾 Dogs communicate with each other using body language. This issue is very relevant with regard to CGC Test Item 8, Reaction to Another Dog. Clothes and costumes can mask the subtle signals that one dog sends to another to communicate. Other than coats needed for harsh weather, you should leave the canine couture at home when your dog is at the dog park or interacting with other dogs. As much as you may like dressing up your dog, remember to keep his canine traits and needs in mind.

Attending a CGC class gives you the added benefit of socialization so that your dog is comfortable around other dogs.

REACTION TO DISTRACTIONS

This test demonstrates that the dog is confident at all times when faced with common distracting situations. The Evaluator will select two distractors from among the following (since some dogs are sensitive to sound and others to visual distractions, it is preferable to choose one sound and one visual distraction):

- A person using crutches, a wheelchair, or a walker (5 feet [1.5m] away).
- A sudden opening or closing of a door.
- Dropping a pan, folded chair, or other object no closer than 5 feet (1.5m) from the dog.
- A jogger running in front of the dog.
- A person pushing a cart or crate dolly no closer than 5 feet (1.5m) away.
- A person on a bike no closer than 10 feet (3m) away.

A note about distractions: Distractions, including gunshots, the rapid opening of an umbrella close to the dog, having the dog walk on a metal grid, and others, are items that may be seen on a temperament test. The AKC has its own temperament test, the AKC Temperament Test (ATT), which tests a dog's reaction to certain stimuli but does not include reaction to gunshots. The CGC Test should not be confused with temperament testing. While CGC instructors may include a variety of distractions (e.g., a person in scuba gear) in training classes, the CGC Test should use distractions that are common occurrences in the community.

- The dog may show casual interest and may appear slightly startled. The dog may jump slightly but should not panic and pull at the leash to get away.
- The dog may attempt to walk forward slightly to investigate the distractor.
- Dogs that become so frightened that they urinate (or defecate) should not pass.
- Dogs that growl or lunge at the distractor should not pass.
- An isolated (one) bark is acceptable. Dogs that continue to bark at the distractor should not pass.

Walking your dog around the neighborhood will expose him to a variety of distractions.

- Handlers may talk to their dogs and give encouragement and praise throughout the test. Handlers may give instructions to their dogs ("Sit, good boy, watch me, etc.").
- Several national therapy dog groups use the CGC as a prerequisite for their evaluations. These groups specify which distractors should be used. Evaluators who conduct these tests for therapy dog organizations will have this information.
- A distraction cannot simply be noise in the background (dogs barking, cars). Distraction stimuli should be consistent for each dog.

The world is full of unpredictable sights, sounds, and moving objects. CGC Test Item 9, Reaction to Distractions, is the test item that assesses your dog's ability to espond appropriately in the presence of distractions.

What Are Distractions?

Distractions are basically just the stimuli (including sights, sounds, people, and things) encountered in the world. Most people think of distractions as those events that divert attention from what a person is doing, such as, "I'm sorry my report is late, but I looked out the window, there was an elephant in the yard, and I could not concentrate."

Distractions can be stimuli or activities that are pleasing and entertaining. For humans, this can be something like a person's going to a movie to get his or her mind off being overloaded with work. When a dog that is being trained in the backyard to perform an off-leash obedience routine runs to the opposite corner of the yard and chases a squirrel, the dog has found a distraction that he considers far more entertaining than what his trainer is asking him to do.

Distractions can also be upsetting stimuli (e.g., things or conditions in the environment) that can cause emotional turmoil or uncertainty or serve as obstacles

to paying attention or completing a behavior. The accountant who is trying to balance a budget might have a difficult time completing the task if there is a worker using a jackhammer outside his office window. The small dog that has nicely walked on leash down the sidewalk of a particular street every day might suddenly notice that balloons have been attached to the railing of an outdoor café, and they

CGC training can help you keep your dog's attention on you in the presence of distractions.

are blowing in the breeze. Not so sure about this new distraction, the little dog plants his feet and decides there is no way, no how, he is walking any farther. How to react appropriately to distractions is one of the most beneficial skills you can teach your dog.

Exposing Your Dog to Distractions

When puppies are nine to twelve weeks old, although an exploratory phase begins weeks before this, they get very serious about exploring new spaces and objects around them. Taken outside at this age, a group of puppies will scatter, each one busier than the next with very important exploring. Pick up a young puppy who is exploring, and he is likely to kick his feet and squirm as if to say, "Put me down! I am very busy right now." Jumping into the tall grass, working to get his roly-poly puppy body up a low step on the porch, and running with unabated joy to any new human who appears are typical puppy behaviors.

It's much easier to bring your dog out and about when he is comfortable around distractions.

If the puppy goes straight from this idyllic existence into a home with an owner who understands the critical importance of continuing to expose the puppy to new experiences (which is basically CGC Test Item 9, Reaction to Distractions), the pup will grow into a dog that is confident and self-assured. Very unfortunately, dogs sometimes don't get that perfect start in life, or they somehow develop fearfulness and other inappropriate reactions to distractions. When this happens, the good news is that, with systematic procedures, dogs at any age can learn to have appropriate reactions to distractions.

The following list of distractions shows some of the many stimuli that your dog will encounter at home and in the community. The list can be used both as (1) an assessment (would your dog have an acceptable reaction to these items?) and (2) a list of exercises that can be used in classes and in training sessions that you do with your dog. There is some overlap in the categories; for example, a stimulus may be listed as both a noise and a motion distraction. The "places" category is listed so you can think about a variety of places that you can take your dog, but the distractions presented (such as noise and visual distractions) in this category are also listed separately. It's important to note that before taking a puppy into the community on a regular basis, he has all necessary vaccines, and your veterinarian has given you the green light to begin daily excursions to new places.

Types of Distractions

People as Distractions

- Immediate family. When you first bring your dog home, he will meet you and the immediate family. Your dog may need a special, slow introduction to certain family members, such as your newborn baby who screams at the top of her lungs, Grandpa with his gruff voice, and your very energetic ten-year-old son.
- All shapes and sizes. People come in all shapes and sizes. Expose your dog to babies, children, men, women, teenagers, older people, people with shrill voices, and people with loud voices. Clothing can present a problem—here at the AKC, we can tell you about a lot of dogs that were disqualified at rainy outdoor shows when they did not want a judge, who happened to be wearing a raincoat and hat, to touch them. In cities, teenagers on skateboards, people walking along with shopping bags, and joggers present your dog with people-related distractions.

Places as Distractions

- Distractions at home. Once your new dog comes home with you, your home will be the place that distractions (i.e., new stimuli) will be introduced. Balls that roll, toys that squeak, a new bed, a crate, doors that slam, and kitchen noises are all distractions in the home. If your dog previously lived outside, he may be nervous when he is first exposed to carpeting, tiled floors, or steps. If your dog previously lived in a kennel, he may be familiar with concrete and gravel surfaces but not grass or dirt. While we don't usually think of dirt as a distraction, the key concept here is that early exposure to a wide variety of stimuli will result in a steady dog that is better able to deal with other kinds of distractions.
- Distractions in the yard. In addition to becoming accustomed to the inside of the house, your dog will find plenty of distractions outside in the yard. Wind blowing, squirrels running along the fence, water in the swimming pool, chimes on the back porch, the neighbor's children playing football, and the noisy lawnmower are some of the distractions he may encounter outdoors.
- Distractions in the community. The community provides an endless source of distractions for dogs. Cars driving by, people and other dogs on busy sidewalks, people playing tennis with a ball like the one the dog has at home, and trips to the vet, the groomer, training classes, and the pet-friendly bistro are all common

distractions in the community. Ideally, your dog will go many places with you. Staying in a pet-friendly hotel provides new experiences, such as concrete stairs and elevators. As your dog reacts acceptably to the common distractions in your neighborhood, you can practice with distractions that are a little more challenging, such as opening and closing an umbrella or having the dog walk on an unusual surface such as wire grating. Helpers in your training class can wear unusual costumes and make strange noises.

Noises

At home, there are plenty of noise distractions. Pots and pans, televisions, radios, washing machines, vacuum cleaners, doorbells, telephones, lawn mowers, doors that slam, and the seventh-grader practicing his trumpet are all examples of noise-related distractions. In public places, such as a park, there will be children laughing and yelling, birds chirping, balls bouncing, and water sounds from fountains and lakes.

Fireworks and thunder are in a category of their own when it comes to noise. In the weeks preceding Fourth of July, animal-control agencies across the country remind people to keep their dogs inside. Dogs that are left in backyards can become so panicked, even traumatized, by fireworks that they dig out of their yards and run away. The best thing you can do to keep your dog safe on Fourth of July is to keep him inside.

Desensitizing a dog to actual fireworks is a little difficult because the training opportunity occurs infrequently. Throughout the rest of the year, you can work with your dog on tolerating a variety of noises so that fireworks are more tolerable.

Some dogs are afraid of thunder, which is more than just a noise problem. Thunder is paired with driving rain, lightning, an increase of static charges in the air, and the ground and windows shaking.

To handle both fireworks and thunderstorms, make sure that your dog knows he is safe. Bring him into the house with you. Close the curtains if there are flashes of lightning paired with the thunder. This is a good time to provide some planned distractions. Noise from a movie on television or music can help. You can play games with your dog or provide another distracting activity.

In a relatively small number of cases, dogs cross the line from simply being afraid of thunder to having full-blown phobias. (A phobia is a fear so extreme that it changes the way the animal functions.) Such a dog, if crated, can go into a frenzy to get out of the crate, biting and breaking his teeth on the crate. Or, he may engage in excessive panting, pacing, and drooling. When the reaction to a stimulus is this severe, the owner needs to work with the dog's veterinarian or an animal behaviorist to address the problem.

Working in a college setting to help reduce the students' stress, these therapy dogs encounter many distractions.

For puppies that have not been exposed to storms, and mildy fearful dogs that do not have potentially dangerous reactions to storms, owners can find recordings of thunderstorm noises. The behavioral principle behind these sound effects is desensitization. Play the storm sounds at a low volume, gradually increasing the volume as the dog becomes comfortable with the noises.

Stationary Visual Distractors

Stationary visual distractors are non-moving things that the dog sees. Furniture and parked wheelchairs (which don't even have to move to be frightening) are examples of stationary visual distractors.

Dogs that are extremely sensitive when it comes to their environments can have negative reactions to anything new. For example, the delivery service just dropped off a large box, and you've placed it in the middle of the living room. Your Whippet puppy, who is highly reactive to visual distractions, starts to enter the room. She stops, stands in the doorway, and nervously looks at the package as if to say, "What is that? That does not belong here, and I'm not going near it!"

Scents

Scents are another category of distractions, and for a dog with an especially good nose, scents can be a problem. Dogs that compete in tracking events follow scent on the ground. Sometimes, such a dog is working a track and, without warning, off he goes! If he picks up the scent of a small animal and has to choose between earning a tracking title and "goin' crittering," he's going to find that critter.

In the community, you may choose to take your dog (who has earned the CGC award) to a lunch with a friend at a dog-friendly bistro. Sitting on the outside patio, you realize how great it is that your dog has learned a reliable down-stay. A server passes by, and the dog stands up, no longer wanting to stay at your feet. The smell coming from a tray of hamburgers presented a scent distraction that competed with the down-stay. Practicing the down-stay and providing your own tasty reward is the trick to dealing with this problem.

Smells that only a dog can appreciate are distractions that you'll find everywhere you go. Decide when it is OK for your dog to sniff and when he needs to walk along with you.

One of the most common instances of scent distraction for your dog is when you take him for a walk. There are you are, trying to take a brisk walk, but it seems as if your dog feels the need to stop and sniff every two steps. You'll have to find a happy balance when it comes to letting your dog sniff on walks. If you provide training and allow sniffing on cue, you'll be able to let the dog sniff sometimes and tell him "Let's walk!" at other times.

Most of the time, scent distractions involve scents that are pleasing to the dog. Every now and then, a dog has an unusual reaction to a person. This can happen when the dog who lives in a smoke-free home meets a heavy smoker, or when a person is wearing strong-smelling aftershave or perfume.

Motion Distractors

Motion distractors are things that are moving; the movement is what causes the dog's reaction. Joggers, children on bicycles and skateboards, shopping carts, moving strollers and moving wheelchairs, crate dollies, balls, cars, and other animals are examples of distractions that can take a dog's attention away from doing what he is supposed to be doing or cause an inappropriate reaction. Motion distractions are particular problems for high-prey-drive dogs, who like to chase.

To address problems with moving distractions, consider the following tips:

- Start with the distraction being still. Walk the dog around the distraction. Chances are, there won't be a problem. The problem is motion. It's when the car moves or the cat runs that the dog's prey drive kicks in and the chase begins.
- Use desensitization. Start with the dog far away from the object and gradually get closer. Or start with the object moving very slowly and gradually increase the speed. (Obviously, you can't practice this with squirrels and cats. Both species are unlikely to cooperate during desensitization exercises with your dog!)
- For example, if tennis balls are a distractor, take your dog, a tennis ball, and a helper outside. Begin practicing CGC skills—heeling on leash, walking in a circle, and so on—with your dog. Have your helper stand at a distance from you, throwing the ball up and catching it. Instruct the helper to slowly and gradually move closer to you and your dog while you continue working with the dog and giving plenty of praise and rewards for paying attention.
- If a fast-moving object is the problem (usually seen in high-prey-drive dogs), you can start by slowing rolling a ball or moving a toy as you tell the dog to stay. Gradually increase the speed of the ball/toy and reward the dog for staying in position.

- In these types of training exercises, be fair to beginning dogs. A dog with an advanced level of training will sit-stay while you throw his favorite tennis ball in the air. For dogs that are just starting their training, use a neutral toy to start. Give your dog every chance to be successful.
- Use DRI techniques. DRI is a particularly effective technique for dogs that chase cars. On leash, the dog is taught to heel, sit, and stay as cars drive by and is rewarded for the appropriate behaviors (that are incompatible with chasing).
- Use a "sit and watch" procedure to control the dog. Ideally, your dog will learn to follow your instructions ("Let's walk," "Sit," "Come," and so on) even when there are moving distractors present. But until the dog is well-trained, a good sit-stay is your friend. You can have your dog sit and watch when distractors are a problem. There is something about having the dog in a sit or down that stops his momentum and decreases the chances that the dog is going to chase the moving distractor.
- As an advanced exercise, in a safe, enclosed area, take your dog off leash. When the dog begins to run toward the distraction, call your dog to come to you (recall). When the dog comes to you, give plenty of praise and a treat.
- Practice around cats, squirrels, and other small animals. Some breeds have been bred for centuries for hunting. It's in their genes. A very well-trained dog can be called off a squirrel, cat, or other small animal. However, until your dog is very well trained, use leashes, fences, and plenty of good sense to keep other animals safe.

SUPERVISED SEPARATION

This test demonstrates that a dog can be left the Evaluator is encouraged to say something like, "Would you like me to watch your dog?"

An Evaluator will hold the dog's leash while the owner goes out of sight for three minutes. Evaluators may talk to and pet the dog but should refrain from giving the dog excessive attention, playing with the dog, etc.

- The dog does not have to stay in position.
- If the dog continually barks, whines, or howls, he should not be passed.
- The dog should not pace unnecessarily and should not show signs of agitation.
- A dog that simply walks back and forth and looks for his handler is passed. There should be no signs of extreme stress, including panting, breathing hard, etc.
- If a dog begins to look very upset or distressed (barking, whining, panting, pacing, pulling), the test should be terminated. The CGC Test is an activity that should be fun. We do not want dogs or handlers to have a bad experience with the CGC. If a dog is extremely distressed, training is needed. (This training should not be done during testing.) This one incident of giving in to the dog's insecure behavior is not enough to cause any lasting effect. The owner should be told nicely that separation is an issue for the dog and that some training would help the dog feel more secure.
- If a dog pulls on his leash (trying to get away), he should not be passed.
- Any dog that urinates or defecates during testing should not be passed. The exception to this is when Test 10 is held outdoors, or between exercises outdoors (e.g., the dog urinates on a bush while being walked to the next test station). Dogs should not stop to relieve themselves while they are working with the handlers in the exercises.

In CGC Test Item 10, the owner leaves the dog with the Evaluator, who may talk to the dog but should not provide too much attention.

As much as we might like to spend every minute of every day with our dogs, there are times when our beloved canine family members need to spend time alone. CGC Test Item 10, Supervised Separation, test your dog's ability to stay with a trusted person for a short period of time. This is the first step toward your dog's tolerating a separation from you.

In the real world, examples of times when you might need another person to watch your dog while you are not in the dog's sight include leaving the dog with at the grooming salon, leaving the dog with the veterinarian while you step out of the room, and stepping away to make a call on your cell phone, go to the restroom, or go into a store. Eventually, your dog will need to stay without you for longer periods of time, such as if he requires an overnight stay at the veterinarian's office or at a boarding kennel.

Teaching CGC Test Item 10

As a prerequisite to the Supervised Separation exercise, a great game for group puppy-training classes is "Pass the Puppy." Everyone sits in a circle and holds his or her puppy. When the instructor gives the cue, everyone passes his or her puppy to the next person. The instructor continues to give the signal to "pass the puppy" until everyone has held every puppy and each person has his or her own puppy back. This exercise exposes puppies to a lot of new people, and they learn at an early age that humans other than their owners will not hurt them.

Some dogs will have no trouble staying with another person, but other dogs, particularly if they have no experience staying with another person, may not want to leave "Mom" or "Dad." If your dog does not want to stay with another person, try the following steps:

1. Stand beside the other person. Hold your dog's leash.
2. Stand close to the other person. Don't leave, but let the other person hold the leash.
3. Stand beside the other person. With the person holding the leash, step back one step and then return to the dog while the other person praises the dog and gives a food reward if the dog will take it. The dog should receive attention only if he is calm.
4. Repeat Step 3 but take two steps away from the dog. Anytime the dog starts whining, pacing, panting, appearing stressed, etc., go back to the previous step.

In a training class, you'll be able to practice for CGC Test Item 10 with your classmates.

In the CGC Test, the owner will leave the dog with the Evaluator and go out of sight for three minutes.

5. Teach this skill systematically, adding one step farther away at a time. The biggest mistake people make is trying to make progress too fast, for example, an owner giving the leash to the helper and then immediately walking across the room to the doorway. This can cause the dog to panic.

6. Once you've worked up to getting across the room, it is time to step outside the door (for one second) and then return. Add a few seconds at a time until you can be gone for three minutes. If a few seconds at a time is too many, add one second at a time.

7. When you return, if the dog acts like you have been gone for twenty years and goes into a hysterical fit of joy (jumping, spinning), be very calm and don't reinforce his excited behavior. Wait until he is calm, then praise and reward the dog.

Unsupervised Separation

Ultimately, in the real world, "supervised separation" will progress to the separation that occurs when you leave your dog unsupervised. You might have heard stories about what can happen when dogs with separation problems are left home alone.

Urinating/Defecating When the Owner Leaves

Some dogs urinate or defecate on the floor every time their owners leave home. For example, Spot was a Dalmatian that would urinate in his owner's bed when his owner left to go to work. We don't mean scent marking, in which a dog sprinkles the corner of the bedspread. Spot got in the bed when Dad went off to work and left a large puddle in the middle of the bed.

Destroying Things When the Owner Leaves

Sometimes, destruction is the primary problem related to separation. Sasha was a beautiful Siberian Husky whose owner did not believe in crate-training or using a kennel. Sasha was free to roam about the house, and in addition to frequently chewing things, on occasion she would pull the curtains down when her owner left.

In training for this test item, leaving your dog with a friendly, dog-savvy person will help the dog adjust to your absence.

Once the drapes were on the floor, Sasha seemed to systematically chew at least one hole in each curtain panel so that all of them needed to be replaced. More than once, Sasha pulled so hard on the curtains that she also pulled the curtain rods out of the wall, requiring drywall repair in addition to replacement curtains.

Noise Related to the Owner's Leaving

Noise is another problem that is often seen (or heard) when dogs have separation issues. One toy-breed owner who liked to travel had four Maltese. When she would stay in a hotel, the dogs were easy to care for, and they were all house-trained. The dogs would be fed, walked, and given personal attention, and then the owner would leave and go out to dinner. As she left the room, the four sweet, angelic darlings had halos over their heads as they watched from their crates. Just about the time that the owner got to the end of the hall and on the elevator, all four dogs started barking. And barking, and barking for hours, disturbing every exhausted traveler who was unfortunate enough to have a room nearby.

Problems for Owners and Property Owners

Urinating and defecating indoors, destroying property, and making enough noise to disturb others are issues that owners face when their dogs have problems related to separation. These are also problems that concern property owners, and they are primary reasons that pets are not permitted in many apartments, condos, and rental houses. Remember the Responsible Dog Owner's Pledge—to protect the rights of pet owners, never let your dog infringe on the rights of others by making excessive noise, inappropriately urinating or defecating indoors, or causing damage to property.

Separation Issues

Separation Anxiety

You may have heard the term "separation anxiety." For quite a while, this has been the term used to refer to problems that dogs have when left alone. Technically, "anxiety" means that there are physiological changes in the animal, such as shortness of breath, heart palpitations, and increased blood pressure and heart rate. There is also usually a certain amount of worrying and apprehension that goes along with the clinical definition of anxiety. A well-recognized type of anxiety with humans is test anxiety, where the person can panic to the point of trembling, feeling sick, and developing a migraine related to an upcoming important exam. Because not all dogs that are left alone experience anxiety, animal behaviorists are beginning to use other terms, including "separation distress" and "separation behaviors."

Separation Distress

Distress is simply an animal's inability to adapt to stress (or the conditions that cause stress). In humans and animals, the results of stress are often maladaptive behaviors that include inappropriate urinating or defecating (toilet-trained children who are experiencing distress might wet the bed or wet their pants), making noise (dogs bark and whine while distressed children might cry), and destruction or aggression. In many situations, separation distress is a more accurate term than separation anxiety.

WHAT REALLY HAPPENED?

Clearly, more research is needed in the area of separation issues. If your dog has separation problems, and you can get video footage of the dog in action, it can help an animal behaviorist know how to best develop a plan of action.

CGC training offers valuable socialization with other dogs and their owners.

Separation Behaviors

Sometimes, a dog owner returns home to discover that toilet paper has been dragged from the bathroom all through the house, and underwear is strewn about the living room. Did a tornado hit the house? No, the dog was at it again. While you were gone, you're certain your dog did a canine imitation of scene in the movie *Risky Business* in which Tom Cruise jumps on the coffee table and plays a broom as if it were a guitar.

There are some differences of opinion about this, but when it comes to the topic of separation issues, some canine experts believe that there are times when the dog is neither anxious nor distressed when the owner leaves, and he is just having a good time with his mischievous behaviors. But the idea that some dogs get bored and start parties when their owners are gone is controversial. What we do know is what happened—toilet paper all over the house, chewed-up shoes, and perhaps even a puddle on the owner's bed. These can all be accurately referred to as separation behaviors. In any case, it is never appropriate to punish a dog for what he did while you were away.

Ten Tips for Leaving Your Dog Alone

1. Shape Behaviors

Remember shaping, in which you start with leaving the dog for a short time and then gradually add time? The mistake that owners often make when they get a puppy or new adult dog is that, once they see that he is doing fine with the new family, they leave him alone all day while they go to work and school. You should leave the dog for only a very short time (e.g., minutes) the first time and see how he responds.

If your dog has a problem related to separation and engages in separation behaviors as soon as you walk out the door, you may need to implement a systematic training procedure. You need to have a block of time for this training—don't start this when you are in a hurry and can only do part of the process. The systematic training looks like this:

- Without making a big deal over leaving, tell the dog, using whatever message you choose, that you are going. You can say something like "I'll be back" or "Watch the house." What you say doesn't matter as long as you use a matter-of-fact tone and say the same thing each time. This will help the dog learn that you are coming back when you say the chosen phrase.
- Walk out the door, close the door, and immediately open the door and return. If the dog gets excited and jumps on you, do not reward his behavior by talking to him or petting him—wait to do this until the dog is calm.
- Repeat the verbal cue you established. Walk out the door, close the door, wait one second, and return. Add a few seconds each time. You may have to do this thirty times before you can start adding minutes.

This process can be time-consuming, and you might find yourself getting bored going in and out the door. Know, however, that when done properly, this is an effective procedure for addressing separation problems.

AKC S.T.A.R. Puppy training is a natural lead-in to the Canine Good Citizen Program.

2. Consider Crate Training

If you get a puppy or dog that has separation problems, and you have to leave the dog alone, the first thing to remember is that you need to keep him safe. A puppy that wanders around the house, chewing electrical cords, or a dog that chews through the back-porch screen can get in a lot of trouble, not to mention danger. There are many books that will teach you how to humanely and safely crate-train your dog. A crate should be large enough that the dog can move around comfortably. When used properly—not overused—a crate can be an effective tool for keeping your dog safe and preventing a disaster.

3. Provide Toys to Prevent Boredom

For real separation distress, you will most likely need to do systematic training as previously described. For dogs that can be loose in the house as well as dogs that are crated during the day, providing them with safe, acceptable toys is a smart move that can help prevent boredom. If you give your dog toys, make sure that the items you choose are not things that can be destroyed (e.g., stuffed animals) and cause problems such as choking or intestinal blockages if swallowed. There is a variety of dog toys in which you can place treats or peanut butter so the dog has to do some work to get the reward. If you choose not to use a crate, be sure to puppy-proof your home before leaving the dog alone so that he doesn't make a bad or dangerous choices (such as chewing your expensive Italian leather shoes or your computer cord).

4. Meet Your Dog's Physical Needs

Before leaving your dog alone for an extended period of time, make sure that you've met all of his physical needs. This includes providing fresh water and taking him out to relieve his bladder and bowels. When a house-trained dog has not been given an adequate bathroom trip before you leave, it can be extremely stressful both physically and mentally for the dog to try to do the right thing by "holding it" until you come home.

5. Exercise Your Dog

Exercise is another of your dog's physical needs. Giving your dog a short walk or a chance to play before you go to work can go a long way toward having a dog that is relaxed and ready to take a rest when you are gone.

6. Keep a Regular Schedule

A predictable schedule can help your dog avoid separation issues. After you've completed your own morning routine, if you let the dog outside for adequate exercise, give him a dog biscuit and fresh water, and say "Watch the house" (or whatever your good-bye cue is) every time you leave, the dog will learn that this is the morning drill. Before long, you'll be home from work, and it will be time for another walk, training, and playtime.

7. Provide Familiar Sounds

Some owners report that their dogs are more relaxed when they hear a familiar sound, such as a television or radio. When the owners leave, they make sure that their dogs have music, the Weather Channel, or some other background noise. Animal shelters also report that dogs seem calmer when music is played in kennel areas.

8. Be Aware of Multiple-Pet Interactions

If you add a puppy or new dog to a household that already has other pets, make sure that you understand the dynamics between the animals before leaving the new dog alone with them. For example, you don't want to leave a large dog with a smaller dog if there is any chance that the small dog will be terrorized or injured, and you don't want to leave a dog with cats unless you are certain that the dog will not attempt to hurt the cats.

9. Divide and Conquer

When you have multiple dogs that bark incessantly while you are away, it will be difficult, or impossible, to change the behavior of a group of dogs. You probably need to divide and conquer to solve this problem, working with one dog at a time to get them all under control. The best solution might be to change your own behavior. For example, let's say you are traveling with your dogs. Instead of leaving them in the hotel room so they can bark and disturb other guests while you go out for dinner, you could take them with you to a dog-friendly café, order room service, or put the dogs in the car and get your dinner from a drive-through. Dogs that bark and disturb others while in hotels and other public places can put the rights of all dog owners at risk.

10. Return Calmly

When you follow the systematic plan (described previously) for leaving your dog, you'll go out the door and then come back in, repeating this multiple times. At first, you'll stay outside the door for just a few seconds at a time, then you'll gradually add more time as the dog responds calmly when you come back into the house. If you come back inside and the dog jumps on you and goes crazy, you've probably increased the amount of time that you are gone too quickly. You'll need to go back to being outside the door for a shorter time.

If you come back into the house and the dog is spinning, trying to jump on you, or otherwise initiating an excited greeting, ignore the dog, even if you have to turn and walk away. When the dog is calm, you can pet him and say hello. The idea here is that you already have a dog that thinks it is terrible if you leave. If you reinforce an excited frenzy when you come back, you are simply confirming for the dog that being separated is a horrible thing.

Feeling Comfortable

Dogs that receive regular training have fewer behavior problems. Training gives a dog something to wrap his mind around. When owners and dogs attend training classes together, they practice new skills each day, and this provides a routine that is very helpful to dogs. Attending a six-week class is the perfect beginning, but if your dog has any signs of separation behaviors, you should continue training beyond the initial introductory class. Consider participating in an AKC sport with your dog such as Rally, obedience, or agility.

CGC Test Item 10, Supervised Separation, begins with teaching your dog to stay with a trusted person for a short period of time. In the context of your daily life with your canine family member, the supervised separation exercise serves as a foundation for a dog that eventually feels comfortable staying home alone and peacefully waiting for your return.

CGC Test Item 10 was created to prevent the separation issues to which dogs can be prone.

THE CGC RESPONSIBLE DOG OWNER'S PLEDGE

The Canine Good Citizen concept applies to both ends of the leash. Every dog that earns the CGC award should have a responsible owner. The Responsible Dog Owner's Pledge is one of the most important parts of the CGC Program. If every dog owner followed this pledge, there would be no need for restrictive legislation pertaining to dogs, there would be far fewer dogs in shelters, and there would be a significant decrease in dog-related problems, such as bites. Responsible dog owners agree to:

- take care of their dogs' health needs;
- ensure that their dogs are safe;
- never allow their dogs to infringe on the rights of others; and
- understand that owning a dog is a commitment in time and caring.

The CGC Responsible Dog Owner's Pledge is signed by each owner before owner and dog are taken through the CGC Test. This chapter explains the Responsible Dog Owner's Pledge.

Dogs want to please us, they really do. With short daily training sessions, all dogs can learn the skills on the Canine Good Citizen Test in a matter of weeks. But passing the CGC Test isn't enough to make a dog a good citizen. For a dog to be well mannered, he needs a responsible owner as a partner. The Responsible Dog Ownership training portion of the CGC Program is perhaps more important than the ten-step test for the dog. Responsible owners will ensure that dogs continue to be welcome members of our communities.

A dog owned by responsible owners is a true member of the family, a friend to those of all ages.

Should You Get a Dog?

The first step to being a responsible dog owner is determining if the time is right for you to have a puppy or dog in your life. When you make the decision to add a puppy to your family, be prepared to look into that puppy's eyes and say, "I'm here for you for the next fifteen years. I will do whatever it takes to care for you, keep you safe, and give you a high-quality life."

Beginning with AKC S.T.A.R. Puppy, CGC training is something the entire family can enjoy.

Are you prepared to house-train a puppy and be patient if there are accidents on your new carpet? Are you prepared to lose sleep during the first weeks that you have your puppy at home because he cries for his littermates and needs to go outside every two hours, even when it's raining? Do you have the time to give your puppy adequate exercise several times a day? Are you prepared to invest the time that it will take to train your puppy to be well behaved? If you have children who are begging for a puppy, is there a responsible adult in the family who is committed to taking care of the puppy and providing him with love and attention if the children become bored with him? If the puppy is intended to be an integral part of a child's life, is there an adult in the home who can teach the child how to properly care for an animal and treat the dog with kindness?

You may decide that you would prefer to adopt a dog that has outgrown puppyhood. Bringing an adult dog into your family also has special considerations. Are you willing to work through any behavioral issues that this dog has developed? If you select a dog from a shelter or rescue group, you may not know the dog's exact medical history. Are you prepared to pay for any unforeseen and perhaps costly medical expenses? If you can't make these long-term commitments, it may not be the right time for you to add a dog to your family.

Choosing the Right Dog for You

You've thought about all the pros and cons of dog ownership. You've searched your soul. You are at a time and place in your life where a dog would be a very positive addition to your family. The next step is determining the right dog for you. Do you want to benefit from the predictable traits of a purebred dog from a responsible breeder, do you want to adopt a dog from a rescue group, or do you want to visit a shelter to find your new dog? If you decide that a purebred dog is for you, educating yourself about individual breeds is your next step.

The approximately 200 AKC breeds are all different. Do you want a big dog or a small dog? Do you want a short-coated dog or a dog with longer hair? Are you looking for a breed that is typically good with children? It is important to match your dog's temperament with the general "temperament" of your family. If you are an active, athletic family, you may not want a breed that is largely inactive. A Basset Hound can be a great dog, but he won't be the world's best jogging companion. If you are a quiet, stay-at-home-and-watch-TV person, you don't need a Border Collie that has been bred for centuries to run all day and find "jobs" to do.

Where Should You Go to Get a Dog?

Now you have some ideas about the type or breed of dog that you're looking for. Where will you get this dog? First, you can get a purebred dog from a responsible breeder. Responsible breeders are well versed in canine genetics. They breed dogs to improve the quality of an individual breed, and they have organized breeding plans. Responsible breeders are involved with their national breed clubs (parent clubs) and are educated about any physical or genetic problems related to their breeds. Responsible breeders will be able to tell you about the past generations in your dog's bloodline, leading up to his breeding. Responsible breeders participate in conformation shows, which are designed to reward dogs that have superior physical structure and screen out those with structural and physical problems. Dogs that do not meet their breed's written standards are not bred.

In most cases, responsible breeders will have homes (and waiting lists) for every puppy months before each litter is born. Litters are planned well in advance, and finding the sire or dam who will be the best match in a mating may involve a dog that lives all the way across the country. A responsible breeder will have done a number

Your first step on the road to responsible ownership is the selection of a puppy from a reputable source.

of health screenings on any dogs to be bred. Some of these screenings include the Orthopedic Foundation for Animals' (OFA) hip dysplasia evaluation, the Canine Eye Registration Foundation's (CERF) tests for eye problems, and thyroid checks.

Most responsible breeders will have contracts, stating that if anything happens in the lifetime of a dog so that the owner can no longer keep him (or if the dog has any problems), the breeder will take the dog back and either care for him or find him a loving home for the remainder of his life. Responsible breeders will want to stay in touch with owners of their dogs so they can hear from time to time how the dogs are doing. Your breeder is available to you as a resource if you have any trouble raising or caring for your dog. Many people find that the breeders of their dogs become their friends and mentors.

This is far different treatment than what you will get if you purchase a dog from a "backyard breeder." Backyard breeders are the local breeders you may see advertising in the newspapers. A backyard breeder usually breeds dogs either to make money, to get a puppy from a dog he or she likes, or to allow his or her children to witness the miracle of birth. When such a breeder decides to breed a dog, the breeder finds a local dog of the opposite sex and same breed—just about any local dog of that breed will do. After purchasing a puppy from a backyard breeder and leaving the premises, the dog is your dog, and any of the dog's problems are yours, too. Buying a dog from such a breeder perpetuates the problem of backyard breeding and uneducated breeders. Backyard breeders often know nothing about the history or characteristics of the breed of dog they're selling.

DID YOU KNOW?

You can find a responsible breeder and a list of purebred rescue groups and read about individual breeds at *www.akc.org.*

Another place to get a dog is from a rescue group. There are breed-specific rescue groups and all-dog rescue groups. Most AKC parent clubs have rescue programs for their breeds (see *akc.org*). Rescue dogs are usually adult dogs, but rescue groups sometimes have puppies. Dogs from rescue groups are loving, wonderful dogs that deserve good homes. Some may have behavioral issues, so you should be prepared to handle these issues and address your new dog's training needs.

Finally, you can go to your local shelter to get a dog. Shelter dogs, like rescue dogs, may have some behavioral issues. Depending on the part of the country in which you adopt a shelter dog, the shelter may not have much, if any, information on the dog's previous owners or living environment. However, carefully selected shelter dogs can make wonderful pets. You can find both purebred and mixed-breed dogs in shelters, and all will benefit from Canine Good Citizen training and loving owners.

Responsible Ownership

The first thing you'll be asked to do when you enter a Canine Good Citizen Test is to complete the registration form and sign the Responsible Dog Owner's Pledge. In signing the pledge, you'll agree to the two primary components of responsible dog ownership: (1) to be responsible for your dog's health needs, safety, and quality of life throughout his life and (2) to never allow your dog to infringe on the rights of others.

Being Responsible for Your Dog's Health Needs
Finding a Good Veterinarian

By signing the CGC Responsible Dog Owner's Pledge, you'll agree to be responsible for the healthcare of your dog. Healthcare includes, first and foremost, selecting a veterinarian and taking the dog in for an initial evaluation and to establish a medical record at the clinic. The veterinarian will work with you, the dog's owner, to determine the most appropriate vaccine schedule for the dog. It was once expected that all dogs would be vaccinated annually; however, there is some debate in the veterinary community regarding vaccines. For this reason, owners and their veterinarians should work together to develop appropriate vaccine plans for individual dogs.

In addition to providing vaccines and medical treatment when needed, your veterinarian can help you develop preventative-care plans that will improve your dog's quality of life. Preventative plans include protecting your dog from internal parasites, such as worms, and external parasites, such as ticks and fleas.

With the increased costs of veterinary care, it is wise to consider health insurance for your dog. You can find helpful information on the health insurance plans offered through the AKC at *www.akcphp.com.*

Providing Adequate Nutrition

Responsible dog owners provide adequate nutrition for their dogs. Adequate nutrition comes from quality dog food with the proper amounts of protein, fat, fiber, vitamins, and minerals. Your dog's breeder or veterinarian can recommend a food, you can learn about dog foods at your local pet-supply store, or you can ask your dog-savvy friends for recommendations. There are specialty foods for puppies, older dogs, and dogs with weight or health problems. Adequate nutrition will help your dog maintain a healthy weight and good coat.

In addition to a good dog food, dogs should have access to clean water at all times. Indoor dogs should always have water in the house. If your dog spends part of the day outdoors, clean water should also be provided outside. Dogs are like humans in that they can get dehydrated when they do not get enough water.

Daily Exercise and Grooming

Daily exercise is needed to keep your dog healthy. Exercise is good for the dog's heart, lungs, circulatory system, and muscles. Regular exercise will play an important part in maintaining your dog's weight and avoiding the many health problems that arise from obesity.

Grooming also plays a role in your dog's good health. Routine grooming tasks, including brushing, bathing, and caring for the feet, nails, eyes, and ears, will keep your dog free from external parasites and skin infections. While bathing should be done on an "as-needed" basis, daily brushing helps your dog's coat maintain good condition. Brushing cleans the coat and stimulates the skin oils that create a healthy shine. Brushing not only improves the coat but also is a way for you and your dog to bond; tactile stimulation is very reinforcing to animals. When brushing doesn't remove the dirt and excess oiliness, it's time for a bath to keep your dog clean.

Being Responsible for Your Dog's Safety

Controlling Dogs with Fences and Leashes

As simple as it seems, leashes and fences are the answers to many of the problems related to dogs in our communities. Even for an avid dog lover, it can be frightening to be walking in the park and have an unknown dog approach at a fast run. Your heart begins to race, and you begin to worry that the dog will bite or attack you or your dog (who is on a leash). Even though you are a dog lover, it is probably still irritating to hear the owner yelling from halfway across the park, "It's OK, he's friendly" (or "He

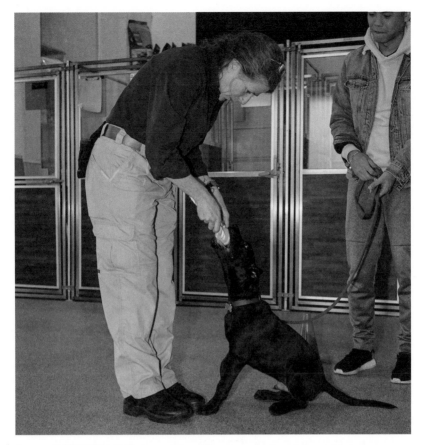

As part of AKC S.T.A.R. Puppy training, this puppy practices giving up his toy on cue.

just wants to say hello," or "He just wants to play."). It doesn't matter if he's friendly. The irresponsible owner and his out-of-control dog doesn't have the right to make others feel uncomfortable or to interrupt other owners' walks with their own dogs.

A responsible dog owner will properly confine or control his or her dog at all times. This involves using leashes in public, fences at home when the dog is outside, and reliable verbal cues when the dog is in an approved off-leash dog area. If you think that a person who is out walking his dog would like his dog to have an opportunity to play with yours, approach the person and ask permission.

Having a fenced yard (or, if you live in the city, taking your dog to a fenced dog park) gives your dog the chance to run and get the gross motor exercise that all dogs need. This kind of exercise cannot be provided with just a walk around the block on a leash. With the exception of geriatric dogs, dogs that have physical problems, or toy breeds that can get much of their exercise indoors, dogs need outdoor exercise in order to expend energy.

DOGS AND CHILDREN

Data clearly shows that most tragic incidents could be prevented if people simply did two things: (1) fenced their dogs and (2) supervised their children. As a responsible owner, a key part of keeping your dog safe is maintaining an environment that sets your dog up for success. Even though parents should supervise their children, it is often the dog that pays the price when there is a dog bite. A dog may be classified as a dangerous dog, with the accompanying restrictions, or, in the worst case, sentenced to mandatory euthanasia.

High-energy breeds are often mistakenly reported by their owners as having behavior problems because they're "hyper." These dogs don't have behavior problems; their owners simply do not understand the level of exercise required for dogs that have been designed to work all day. For example, a Border Collie owner complained about her dog's inability to settle down in the house. She said, "Yes, he gets exercise. I walk him around the block every day when I get home from work." This owner's response underlines why responsible dog owners must take it upon themselves to become well educated about their breeds. If this owner truly understood Border Collies, she would know that she could walk her dog around the block five times and he wouldn't even be warmed up.

Sometimes, even when owners try to be responsible, dogs just don't cooperate. So you follow the AKC's advice and get a brand-new chain-link fence. The dog digs out of the fence, the dog jumps over the fence, or the dog does something that you've never before seen a dog do—he climbs the fence. Now what? If you have a canine Houdini on your hands, you'll have to do your best to dog-proof your fence with extra height at the top and/or concrete reinforcement at the bottom. However, the best solution is to train the dog so that he responds to your verbal cues, engage him in activities, and provide supervision when he is in the yard. If you have to leave, bring the dog into the house. This also prevents someone from stealing your dog, the dog from barking and disturbing the peace while you are gone—or getting bored and digging a tunnel to freedom.

If your dog is destructive, he should be crate-trained to stay in the house when you are gone. You'll rest easy knowing that your dog is in a climate-controlled environment and that he can't get into trouble. A crate provides safety for both your dog and your belongings.

Some owners who don't have fences decide they want a large dog but don't want the dog in the house. Their answer to keeping the dog outside is to chain their pet to a stake. This is not a good idea. Dogs are companion animals. They want to be with you. It is inhumane to have a dog living alone in the yard with no human contact most of the time. If your goal is to have a dog for protection, and you are thinking of chaining your dog outside, invest in a good electronic alarm system instead of a dog. Dogs that are chained for long periods of time can become seriously aggressive. Also, chaining a dog does not protect the child who may wander up to pet the dog.

Identification

As a responsible dog owner, you will do your best to supervise your dog and keep him on your own property. Unfortunately, no matter how hard you try, sometimes accidents happen. For example, the front door is open and your black Lab looks out and sees a squirrel across the street—in a flash, he's gone. Or a friend comes to visit, and her child is playing in the backyard. Too late, you realize that your Whippet was in the yard, and the child left the gate open. For times like these, because accidents happen, you should use some form of identification for your dog to maximize his chances of being returned home.

Collar tags are readily available and inexpensive forms of dog identification. The downsides of collar tags are that they can fall off or break off, the dog may not be wearing his collar when he makes the great escape, and a collar that is worn all the

The behaviors taught in CGC training help keep dogs safe and happy.

time can be a safety hazard if it gets caught on something. Further, if a dog is stolen, his collar tags will be simply removed and thrown into the nearest trash bin, giving you no proof of ownership if you locate your dog.

Microchips and tattoos are good permanent forms of identification. Many veterinarians will microchip or tattoo dogs. Using microchips to permanently identify dogs, the AKC Reunite (formerly AKC Companion Animal Recovery or AKC CAR) program has reunited more than 500,000 lost pets with their owners. Founded in 1995, AKC Reunite has enrolled more than seven million pets.

A microchip is the size of a grain of rice, and each microchip is encoded with a unique and unalterable identification number. The chip is typically implanted just under the skin in the scruff of the dog's neck and lasts for the life of the pet. If your dog has a microchip and is lost, the dog can be scanned at a shelter or participating veterinary clinic to determine if a microchip is present. If the animal is enrolled in the AKC Reunite program, the owners will be notified immediately.

The 100,000th dog to be reunited with her family after being lost was Belle, a puppy whose nose and sense of adventure led her out of her yard and away from home. Belle belonged to the Akowski family in Tucson, Arizona. The Akowskis had Belle microchipped shortly after bringing her home from the animal shelter. As closely as the Akowskis watched Belle, the day came when someone accidentally left a gate open. Belle followed her canine sibling—a known escape artist—out of the yard. Belle got lost, and a kind person eventually found her covered in cactus spines and brought her to a veterinarian, where she was scanned and identified. Someone from the vet's office called AKC Reunite, and the Akowskis were contacted shortly thereafter. Belle was safely returned to her family after an adventure that lasted thirteen days. Without the microchip, Belle might not have been reunited with her family.

Being Responsible for Your Dog's Quality of Life
Basic Training
Responsible dog owners understand that basic training is beneficial to all dogs. Training maximizes dogs' abilities, and, through training, owners enhance their relationships with their dogs. Animal shelter data show that over 90 percent of dogs surrendered to shelters by their owners have had no training. This is an indication that training results in the bonding that makes an owner committed to the dog.

When your dog is under control and responds to cues such as sit, come, down, and stay, you've given your dog the skills he needs to have additional freedom. Canine Good Citizen training is the foundation for all other training that follows in your dog's life. Every dog deserves at least the training required to earn the Canine Good Citizen award. In a one-hour class that meets weekly for six to eight weeks, with about fifteen minutes of practice at home each day, you and your dog can earn the CGC certificate, which shows your ability to teach your dog new skills and your commitment to being a responsible dog owner.

Attention and Playtime

Like young children, puppies learn about the world around them through play. The love of play will continue into your dog's senior years if you make games and playtime fun, reinforcing events. Having your dog run to fetch a ball or soft Frisbee or find things that you've hidden are examples of games that will provide exercise, fun, and mental stimulation for your dog. Every day should include some playtime during which you and your dog can enjoy each other.

A Commitment of Time and Caring

Owning a dog is a commitment. If you provide your dog with quality care, basic training that begins with the CGC skills, daily playtime, and plenty of attention, your dog will become the kind of companion and friend who can make you happy every day.

You are in charge of your dog's quality of life. Dog trainers often say that "people get the dog they deserve," and it seems to be true. Dogs are wonderful, remarkable creatures; they give us their love and devotion, and they deserve no less than responsible, committed owners in return.

Never Allowing Your Dog to Infringe on the Rights of Others

No Running Loose

A key part of being a responsible dog owner is never letting your dog infringe on the rights of others. Dogs should never be permitted to run loose in a neighborhood. When some dog owners are irresponsible, other dog owners lose their privileges, and in a growing number of locations, the privileges lost may include the right to own a dog.

No Nuisance Barking

We all want our neighborhoods to be peaceful places where we can enjoy the restful havens that our homes provide. It is hard to relax or sleep when there is a constantly yapping dog nearby. Responsible dog owners do not permit their dogs to disturb others by engaging in excessive barking.

Dogs of all sizes need training, and CGC training is a wonderful way for them to learn.

If your dog is a barking fanatic, consider a behavior program to put barking "on cue," meaning that the dog learns both "bark" and "no-bark" cues.

Picking Up Waste

When dogs defecate in public places such as parks, hiking trails, and wilderness areas, and their owners do not clean up after them, the first response of city, county, or park officials is to say, "That's it! No more dogs."

Cleaning up after your dog is the right thing to do. Other people enjoy clean recreation spaces, and they should not have to look at or step in your dog's waste. Responsible dog owners carry plastic bags with them on walks and hikes. If your dog soils in a public area, use a bag to clean up after him. You can dispose of the bag in the nearest garbage can.

CGC Responsible Dog Owner's Pledge

I understand that to truly be a Canine Good Citizen, my dog needs a responsible owner. I agree to maintain my dog's health, safety, and quality of life. By participating in the Canine Good Citizen Test, I agree:

I will be responsible for my dog's health needs. These include:
- ✓ routine veterinary care including check-ups and vaccines
- ✓ adequate nutrition through proper diet; clean water at all times
- ✓ daily exercise and regular bathing and grooming

I will be responsible for my dog's safety.
- ✓ I will properly control my dog by providing fencing where appropriate, not letting my dog run loose, and using a leash in public.
- ✓ I will ensure that my dog has some form of identification (which may include collar tags, tattoos, or a microchip ID).
- ✓ I will provide adequate supervision when my dog and children are together.

I will not allow my dog to infringe on the rights of others.
- ✓ I will not allow my dog to run loose in the neighborhood.
- ✓ I will not allow my dog to be a nuisance to others by barking while in the yard, in a hotel room, etc.
- ✓ I will pick up and properly dispose of my dog's waste in all public areas such as on the grounds of hotels, on sidewalks, parks, etc.
- ✓ I will pick up and properly dispose of my dog's waste in wilderness areas, on hiking trails, campgrounds, and in off-leash parks.

I will be responsible for my dog's quality of life.
- ✓ I understand that basic training is beneficial to all dogs.
- ✓ I will give my dog attention and playtime.
- ✓ I understand that owning a dog is a commitment in time and caring.

Owner's Signature_____   Date_____

FINDING CGC TRAINING AND TESTING NEAR YOU

Benefits of CGC Training

The benefits of owning a dog that has passed the Canine Good Citizen Test are many. By teaching your dog the CGC skills and earning the CGC title:

- ❧ you will be the proud owner of a dog that responds to your instructions and is easier to manage;
- ❧ you will have identified yourself as a responsible owner;
- ❧ in CGC classes, you will be introduced to the wonderful world of dog training and all of the exciting activities that come after CGC, such as therapy-dog work, tricks training, Rally, obedience, and agility;
- ❧ depending on where you live, you may have additional privileges, such as admission to dog parks, discounts at veterinary offices, homeowner's insurance benefits, and the ability to participate in therapy-dog groups because of your dog's CGC status; and
- ❧ perhaps most important of all, through CGC training you will develop a bond with your dog that will last forever.

When you arrive to take the Canine Good Citizen Test, you'll find designated areas for each exercise.

The first step is to teach your dog the skills on the Canine Good Citizen Test. If you know how to train dogs, you can teach the skills yourself and then find an AKC Approved CGC Evaluator to test your dog. Or you can attend a training class. Some classes will be called "Canine Good Citizen" classes, but a basic obedience-training class can also prepare you for the CGC Test. All you have to do is tell your instructor at the beginning of the course that passing the CGC Test is a goal.

We strongly suggest attending a class to teach your dog the CGC skills. In a class, dogs will have opportunities for socialization that they won't have if you train on your own. You'll be able to practice the meeting strangers and distraction-dog exercises with other people and their dogs. This experience is invaluable when it comes to teaching your dog to be steady around other people, other dogs, and distractions.

MEET YOUR EVALUATOR

You know that to earn the Canine Good Citizen award, dogs must pass the CGC Test. The test must be administered by an AKC Approved CGC Evaluator. Evaluators are experienced dog trainers. To be approved as an Evaluator, the applicant must have at least two years' experience teaching other people and their dogs, be at least eighteen years old, be in good standing with the AKC, and have experience working with a variety of breeds and types of dogs.

Choosing the Right Instructor for You and Your Dog

Dog training has changed tremendously in the last several decades. Whereas dogs and horses were once trained with heavy-handed punishment-based procedures, current training philosophies are aimed at using positive reinforcement and scientifically based procedures. What seems to vary from trainer to trainer is the extent and level of positive reinforcement and whether corrections are used in training (and, if so, what type).

Many people who decide to take their dogs to classes have seen advertisements or have heard about classes in their area. They register for a class, and they show up on the first night with their dogs. This is not the best way to start a dog-training class. When you are ready to enroll your dog in a training class, we strongly suggest that you call several instructors and ask if you can come and observe before you sign up. Go to the class without your dog, sit and watch the other students, and take note of how the instructor teaches. Many people would have made different choices about their training classes if they had observed the instruction firsthand before enrolling.

The goal is for you to find a class, a training school, and an instructor with a philosophy that is suited to who you are and how you want your dog to be

You can be proud of your dog's CGC achievement and the commitment you've made to his training.

trained. Obviously, you'll want to find a competent instructor, but you also should be on the lookout for a person who will treat you and your dog with the care and respect you deserve.

When you meet an instructor, ask him or her some questions. Examples of questions include:

- How long have you been training dogs?
- What kinds of classes do you teach?
- Have you put any titles on your own dogs?
- What dog sports do you participate in or have you participated in?
- What is your basic philosophy of training?
- What kind of equipment will we be using in class (e.g., collars, etc.)?
- Do you use food rewards? Corrections? If so, can you tell me about these?
- Are all sizes of dogs together in class?

- Do you know your dropout rate? How many students graduate from your classes?
- After the beginning class, do many students go on for additional training?

When you observe the instructor, think about the following:

- The instructor's skill level in teaching humans.
- The instructor's knowledge of dogs.
- The instructor's communication style with students—pleasant and reinforcing, or bossy and sarcastic?
- The organization of the class, i.e., how long is spent on each topic, how many dogs/owners, etc.?
- The curriculum—does it teach all you want to learn?
- The attitude of the dogs—do they look happy and eager to work, or do they seem bored or nervous?
- The attitude of the human students—are they enthusiastic or are they frustrated?
- The way that the instruction is presented and sequenced—is the class set up in such a way to encourage success?
- The teaching methods—do you spend the entire class listening to the instructor talk, or do you get enough time to practice with your dog?
- The instructor's ability to handle any behavior problems or student questions.

Retesting

Some dogs do not pass the CGC Test on the first attempt. If your dog does not pass the CGC Test the first time, don't be embarrassed or disappointed. This could mean that you have a dog that is somewhat challenging to train, or it could mean that you just need to work on a specific behavior a little longer. The important thing is that you've committed yourself to being a responsible owner, you love your dog, and you are working to earn the CGC award. In the grand scheme of things, it won't matter how much training the dog needed.

AKC FAMILY DOG:
BEFORE AND AFTER CGC

The AKC Family Dog Program is a comprehensive good-manners program for all dogs, and the activities build upon and extend CGC training. AKC Family Dog is the organizational umbrella for programs that teach family members how to best communicate with their dogs. The activities are non-competitive, and everyone who trains their dog is a winner. AKC Family Dog includes the following programs: AKC S.T.AR. Puppy, Canine Good Citizen, AKC Community Canine, AKC Urban CGC, AKC Trick Dog, CGC-Ready (for dogs trained by shelters and rescues), AKC Therapy Dog, AKC FIT DOG, and the AKC Temperament Test.

The heart of the AKC Family Dog Program is Canine Good Citizen training, and CGC is the place to go to teach your dog basic canine manners and to learn how to be a responsible dog owner. Hopefully, Canine Good Citizen training will be only one important part of the education that you and your dog experience together. Both before and after CGC, the American Kennel Club is ready with a rich menu

The puppy level of Canine Good Citizen training is an exciting program called AKC S.T.A.R. Puppy.

of training opportunities to help you have a lifetime of learning and fun with your canine companion.

If you've purchased this book, and you have a puppy that is too young for CGC training, that's OK. You can get started in the AKC S.T.A.R. Puppy Program. After CGC, you can go on to train for advanced CGC titles, which include AKC Community Canine and AKC Urban CGC. Other options, once you've become hooked on training, are AKC Trick Dog, AKC Therapy Dog, and competitive activities such as Rally, obedience, and agility.

Before CGC
AKC S.T.A.R. Puppy™

The AKC S.T.A.R. Puppy Program is an exciting program designed to get dog owners and their puppies off to a good start. S.T.A.R. is an acronym for all of the things puppies need to have a good life—Socialization, Training, Activity, and a Responsible owner. The AKC S.T.A.R. Puppy Program is an incentive program for caring dog owners who have taken the time to go through a basic training class that is at least six weeks long with their puppies.

We know that classes are a very effective way to teach owners to communicate with their puppies. Classes provide the knowledge that owners need to raise a puppy, including information on house-training, chewing, and the most practical way to teach basic skills, such as coming when called. The AKC S.T.A.R. Puppy Program is a natural lead-in to the Canine Good Citizen Program.

When you and your puppy complete an AKC S.T.A.R. Puppy class, your puppy is eligible to be enrolled in the AKC S.T.A.R. Puppy Program. Your instructor will administer the twenty-item AKC S.T.A.R. Puppy Test at the end of the course. Upon passing the test, you'll send in your application for enrollment in the program. Your puppy will receive the AKC S.T.A.R. Puppy medal and be listed in the AKC S.T.A.R. Puppy records. You can find more information on the AKC S.T.A.R. Puppy Program can be found at *www.akc.org/starpuppy*.

A proud group of Patriot Service Dogs trainees after earning their CGCA titles.

After CGC
AKC Community Canine™

AKC Community Canine is an advanced CGC program. In AKC Community Canine, dogs who pass the ten-step AKC Community Canine test can earn the CGCA (advanced CGC) title. The goal of AKC Community Canine is to test the dog's skills in a natural setting. For example, rather than testing the dog in a ring at a dog show, the "walks through a crowd" test item involves the dog walking through a real crowd at a dog show, on a busy sidewalk, at a training club, or in a local park. For more information and a copy of the AKC Community Canine test items, see *www.akc.org/products-services/ training-programs/canine-good-citizen/akc-community-canine.*

Part of the Urban CGC test evaluates dogs' ability to walk in public places while staying under control.

AKC Urban CGC™

As with the CGC and AKC Community Canine programs, AKC Urban CGC also requires that the dog pass a ten-step test to earn the Urban CGC title. AKC Urban CGC is more advanced than CGC, and the dog must demonstrate CGC skills and beyond in a setting that includes traffic, crowds, noises, smells, and other distractions that are present in a city or town. The AKC Urban CGC Program shows that dogs are well-behaved when in public settings. This test can be used by dog-friendly businesses (e.g., lodging, retail, transportation, public facilities) to recognize and accept dogs with good manners. For more information and a list of test items, see *www.akc.org/products-services/training-programs/canine-good-citizen/akc-urban-canine-good-citizen/about.*

Volunteer trainers work with shelter dogs on their good manners to prepare them for adoption.

CGC-Ready™

CGC-Ready is basically the Canine Good Citizen Program when it is implemented in settings where staff or volunteer trainers train dogs either for their current owners or to prepare them for adoption. CGC-Ready is used by rescue organizations, shelters, prison-based dog training programs, service dog trainers, dog daycare, and boarding kennels that offer training.

In the CGC-Ready Program, dogs are trained by trainers. When a dog is ready, the new owner takes the dog through the CGC Test. In adoption-oriented settings, such as shelters, being ready to pass the CGC Test could mean that the dog is adopted faster.

Therapy dog programs in schools and libraries help engage young readers.

AKC Therapy Dog™

The purpose of the AKC Therapy Dog program is to recognize dogs and their owners who help others by volunteering as a therapy team. Dogs are registered or certified through qualified, recognized therapy dog organizations. AKC Therapy Dog titles can be earned based on the number of visits the dog has completed. For more information, see *www.akc.org/sports/ title-recognition-program/therapy-dog- program/the-purpose-of-this-program.*

Zuke, a therapy dog, virtually visits a friend during the COVID-19 pandemic.

AKC FIT DOG clubs help owners achieve their fitness goals while keeping their dogs active.

AKC FIT DOG™

Now more than ever, fitness is important for both dogs and people. The AKC FIT DOG Program has adopted the American Heart Association's recommendation of walking for a minimum of 150 minutes per week (in 30- to 40-minute sessions). In AKC FIT DOG, owners who meet the fitness requirements and provide documentation can earn a free magnet with the AKC FIT DOG logo. Thousands of owners and dogs have taken and  succeeded at the AKC FIT DOG challenge, and there are now several hundred AKC FIT DOG clubs. To find out how you and your dog can get started on the path to fitness, see *www.akc.org/sports/akc-family-dog-program/akc-fit-dog*.

AKC Trick Dog™

Going all the way back to the days of black-and-white television with *Lassie* and *Rin Tin Tin*, tricks training has been and continues to be one of the most fun and exciting areas of dog training. In the AKC Trick Dog Program, dog owners teach their dogs tricks, or they go to a tricks class. When ready, dogs are tested at five different levels and can earn AKC Trick Dog titles that include Novice Trick Dog, Intermediate Trick Dog, Advanced Trick Dog, Trick Dog Performer, and Trick Dog Elite Performer. Trick dog testing is administered by CGC Evaluators, and tests may be conducted in person or via video.

In 2019, Gryff, a Golden Retreiver owned by Tracy Dulock from Robinson, Texas, was the top trick dog when he won the AKC's first national trick dog competition.

The AKC Temperament Test is held in conjunction with AKC events.

AKC Temperament Test (ATT™)

The AKC Temperament Test (ATT) assesses how a dog reacts to a variety of stimuli. ATT Evaluators watch for desirable traits in the dog, including emotional stability, cooperation with the handler, being appropriately social for his breed, and demonstrating the ability to recover when startled. In the ATT, dogs should not show signs of fear or aggression.

Developed by Mary Burch and Doug Ljungren, the ATT is the first comprehensive prescriptive temperament test. Historically, temperament tests have been thought of in terms of predictive tools. The ATT tests dogs in six categories that include social, auditory, visual, tactile, proprioceptive, and an unexpected stimulus. For more information on the ATT, see *www.akc.org/ akctemptest*.

OTHER FUN TRAINING

Conformation

In conformation dog shows, the emphasis lies on the conformation, or physical structure, of the dog. Dogs are judged on qualities including body structure, general appearance, gait, and temperament. After examining each entry, the dog-show judge decides how closely, in his or her opinion, the dog measures up to that judge's mental image of the perfect dog as described in the breed's written standard.

In conformation, dogs compete for points toward their championships. It takes fifteen points to become a champion of record, and the points must be won under at least three different judges.

Programs for handlers and judges foster professionalism and ethics in those who participate in conformation showing.

At an all-breed show (where all AKC breeds can enter), each Best of Breed winner competes for four placements within his Group. In the final competition, seven dogs (the first-place winners from each Group) compete for Best in Show.

Dogs in conformation shows may not be spayed or neutered. The purpose of conformation competition is to improve purebred dogs by identifying those that are quality representatives of their breeds and thus desirable for breeding.

Junior Showmanship

Junior Showmanship is the AKC activity that teaches young people between the ages of nine and eighteen how to exhibit dogs at shows and develop good sportsmanship. In

Junior Showmanship, the competition is judged solely on the skills of the young handlers, not on the dogs' actual conformation. Juniors may also complete with their dogs in Companion Events (such as obedience and agility) and Performance Events. There is no minimum age for young people who wish to compete in Companion Events.

Agility and ACT

If you didn't blink, you might have seen agility on television. Agility is the fast-paced sport in which dogs run at top speed around a course with equipment that includes tunnels, tire jumps, weave poles, bar jumps, broad jumps, the dog walk, the A-frame, the seesaw, and the pause table.

Dogs in agility are judged on both speed and accuracy, and all breeds and mixed breeds can participate. Because agility is an extremely physical and athletic activity, it is important for both handlers and dogs to receive proper training. Agility is a good source of exercise for active dogs and a great confidence builder for shy, timid dogs.

If you think you might be interested in agility, take a look at ACT, the Agility Course Test. ACT 1 is an entry-level agility event that is designed for the beginning dog to demonstrate sequencing and performance skills. ACT 2 requires the dog to perform additional obstacles.

Obedience

Obedience training provides dogs with a basic education that will help them be better companions. With their ability to follow instructions and their understanding of many cues, obedience-trained dogs excel at other canine sports. AKC obedience clubs across the country can help you train your dog to be a better family pet or to compete in obedience competitions.

AKC obedience is divided into several levels for competition. Novice, Open, and Utility are the three basic levels in which dogs can earn obedience titles. The skills in Novice obedience are more advanced versions of many of the skills on the AKC Canine Good Citizen Test. At each level, the dog needs three qualifying scores (at least 170 out of 200 points) under three different judges to earn the available title at that level. If your dog has the Canine Good Citizen title, a great place to start in AKC obedience is with the Beginner Novice class. Beginner Novice expands on what dogs have learned in CGC, and the exercises include Heel on Leash, Figure Eight, Sit for Exam, Sit/Stay, and Recall (coming when called). All of the exercises in Beginner Novice are performed on leash with the exception of the Recall.

The Labrador Retriever Club of the Potomac awards new recipients of the CGC and AKC Trick Dog titles.

Rally

AKC Rally is one of the AKC's most popular sports, and both dogs and their owners give it rave reviews! Rally is a good next step after AKC Canine Good Citizen. In Rally, the handler/dog team enters the ring and, after instructions from the judge to begin, move at their own pace through a series of signs that designate exercises to be performed. Examples of directions on Rally signs include "Stop and Down," "Moving Down and Walk Around Dog," "90-Degree Pivot Right," and "Leave Dog, Two Steps, Call to Heel and Forward." The handler can communicate with the dog throughout the course by talking, clapping, and giving praise. In cases where there is a tie score on accuracy, the tie is broken by the speed with which the handler/dog teams completed the course.

Tracking

AKC tracking is the activity that teaches dogs to track and follow human scent. You might have seen K9 police officers (in real life or in a movie) using their dogs to track a lost child or a suspect who has run into the woods.

There are four main tracking titles that can be earned. The first is Tracking Dog (TD), in which the dog must follow a track from 440 to 500 yards (402 to 457m) long with three to five changes of direction. Each track is aged for thirty minutes to two hours before the test starts. The Tracking Dog Excellent (TDX) title requires the dog to complete a track that is three to five hours old and 800 to 1000 yards (732 to 914m) long with five to seven changes of direction. In TDX, there are cross-tracks, meaning that a person makes the dog's job of following the track more difficult by walking across the original track.

The Variable Surface Tracking (VST) test is a test of credibility, verifying the dog's ability to recognize and follow human scent while adapting to changing scenting conditions over different surfaces (such as a parking lot, around a building, and down an alley). The Tracking Dog Urban (TDU) test assesses the dog's ability to follow a track laid by a person under a variety of scenting conditions in an urban environment.

Performance Events

The AKC's Performance Events showcase purebred dogs in the jobs that they were originally bred to do. Earthdog tests, herding, lure coursing, field trials, hunt tests, and scent work are the events that make up the AKC's Performance Events.

AKC Performance Events are the events in which dogs demonstrate their inherent abilities to perform the functions they were bred to do. They are judged on their performance and how well they accomplish their task. Many of the breeds participating in Performance Events have high energy, drive, and athleticism and were developed to help bring food to the table. There are various types of performance events geared toward breed-specific eligibility. Lure coursing trials are open to all sighthounds; small terriers and other go-to-ground breeds participate in earthdog, and herding tests and trials are open mainly to herding breeds. There are three main sporting categories for field trials and hunt tests: retrievers, pointing breeds, and spaniels. Scenthounds such as Beagles, Basset Hounds, Dachshunds, and Coonhounds complete in field trials, where they get to show off their tracking skills. Scent work is open to all breeds, as all breeds have the ability to detect scent—though some breeds are naturally more adept than others.

Earthdog Tests

Earthdog tests are for dogs that can "go to ground." Small terrier breeds and Dachshunds were originally bred to go into the dens, holes, or dirt tunnels of underground quarry, such as rats or badgers. The long, low shape of many of the breeds that participate in earthdog events is well suited for crawling into and getting out of tunnels. Today, these breeds are still using their instincts to hunt quarry in tunnels and earning titles at three levels: Junior Earthdog, Senior Earthdog, and Master Earthdog.

Herding Tests/Trials and Farm Dog Certified

The instinct to herd is a result of careful breeding dating back more than a century. Herding tests are simple, non-competitive events in which dogs are judged against a performance standard to evaluate their abilities. There three kinds of herding tests—Herding Instinct (HIC, certificate), Herding Tested (HT, title), and Herding Pre-Trial (PT, title)—each designed for dogs to demonstrate rudimentary skills required for herding. Herding trials are competitive events in which dogs are tasked with having to herd a particular livestock, such as sheep/goats, ducks, or cattle, across a specified type of course at one of three difficulty levels: started, intermediate, or advanced. Titles can be earned for each course type, difficulty level, and livestock type. Both tests and trials require a close working relationship between dog and handler. Many handlers use the testing experience as a precursor to entering trials.

The Farm Dog Certified test is sometimes described as "CGC for farm dogs." The test has twelve exercises that are similar to situations a dog would encounter on a farm. The dog greets the judge, walks on a loose lead through a prescribed pattern, jumps on a hay bale on command, walks by livestock and over unusual surfaces, and passes through a gate. There is a supervised separation exercise, and the dog must also remain under control while farm animals are fed. Reactions to another dog and noises are tested; there is a physical exam (to simulate the handler checking for foreign material, such as burrs), and the dog must behave appropriately when around livestock. Dogs that successfully meet the requirements can apply for the FDC title.

Lure Coursing Tests and Trials

Lure coursing is the fun-to-watch event in which dogs follow an artificial lure around a course across an open field. The lure (that often looks like a white handkerchief) is attached to a wire and is moved mechanically at varying speeds. The dogs see the lure move, their centuries-old hardwiring kicks in, and the chase begins.

Sighthounds were developed to be able to visually follow and physically chase down prey at high speeds over uneven landscapes with twists and turns. These high-powered yet graceful dogs run together in a pack of three during trials and compete for Senior Courser, Master Courser, and Field Champion titles. They are judged on how well they can follow the course. Lure coursing tests are non-competitive and measure a dog's ability to follow, or course, the lure as in the Junior Courser test (JC, title), in which dogs run alone, or in the Qualified Courser test (QC, certificate), in which they must show that they can run with another hound.

The AKC also offers the Coursing Ability Test (CAT) and Fast Coursing Ability Test (Fast CAT). The Coursing Ability Test (CAT) gets you started in lure coursing. Each dog runs individually and chases after a lure on either a 300-yard (274m) or 600-yard (549m) course. The courses are designed for non-sighthound breeds, as CAT is open to all dogs and is graded as pass/fail. Four different CAT titles can be earned, depending on the number of passes. The entry-level title is called the CA, and the dog needs three CAT passes.

Fast CAT is a fun and fast event open to all dogs. Each dog runs a 100-yard (91m) dash down a straight track, chasing a lure, and is timed. Fast CAT is pass/fail only, and three titles can be earned based on accrued points and passes. The faster a dog goes, the more points earned!

Field Trials and Hunt Tests

Field trials and hunt tests are both used to measure a dog's hunting skills by simulating real hunting situations in the field. Hunt tests are non-competitive and offer three suffix titles at each testing level: Junior, Senior, and Master. Field trials are more challenging, are competitive, and offer prefix Field Champion titles.

Separate events are held for Beagles, Basset Hounds and Dachshunds; pointing breeds; retrievers; and spaniels. This is because each of these breeds originally had a slightly different purpose and style when working. All the sporting breeds were bred to hunt, but they work in different ways, and the differences are quite interesting. For

example, spaniels "flush" game (drive it out of cover), whereas pointing breeds will "point" to mark the game. If you have a sporting breed, watching your breed work in the field is a joy.

Scent Work

In the sport of scent work, a dog performs odor searches via cotton swabs that have been saturated with essential oils such as birch, anise, clove and cypress. The swabs are hidden, and the dog must find them and then indicate the find to the handler. Dogs complete searches in several environments, called elements: container, interior, exterior, and buried. There are also several difficulty levels per element: Novice, Advanced, Excellent, Master. Dogs also perform Handler Discrimination searches in which they must locate articles with their handlers' scent. Dogs can earn titles for each element and difficulty level in three concentrations: Odor Discrimination, Handler Discrimination, and Detective. The exciting thing about scent work is that the dog (and the dog's nose) is in control because the handler has no way of knowing where a scent is hidden. Dogs can train for scent work at home or in a class.

SPECIAL APPLICATIONS OF THE CGC PROGRAM

In a relatively short period of time, the AKC's Canine Good Citizen Program has become far more than a ten-item test. This chapter describes some of the many special applications of the Canine Good Citizen concept.

In 1989, the American Kennel Club introduced the Canine Good Citizen Program to reward responsible dog owners and to recognize well-mannered dogs. No one dreamed that, since that time, the CGC Program would dramatically influence the expectations that our culture has regarding the manners of our canine family members. In a growing number of widely diverse settings, the Canine Good Citizen Program is being adopted as a universal standard of behavior for dogs everywhere.

Izzy, of the United States Department of Agriculture's Beagle Brigade, proudly wore her CGC tag.

The Beagle Brigade also includes Labs who have passed the CGC Test.

Animal Control

One of the many jobs of animal-control agencies is to enforce ordinances that pertain to animals. Many ordinances are created to handle problems such as dogs that injure other people or animals, act in a threatening manner, bark incessantly, or otherwise infringe on the rights of others, as well as owners who do not clean up after their dogs in public places.

Depending on the nature of the violation, ordinances range from requiring dogs to wear muzzles to mandating that owners attend training classes with their dogs. An increasing number of animal-control agencies are requiring Canine Good Citizen training (followed by passing the CGC Test) as a rehabilitative measure for dogs and their owners.

Certainly, CGC training alone will not fix a dog with an aggression problem. But, in these cases, it shows that the owner is willing to make a good-faith effort to get the dog under control. Further, the owner signs the Responsible Dog Owner's Pledge, agreeing to properly confine and control the dog.

Detector Dogs

The United States Department of Agriculture's National Detector Dog Training Center (NDDTC) has used the CGC Program as part of its training for detector dogs. Located in Orlando, Florida, the NDDTC trains airport Beagles as well as cargo and border dogs. The CGC Program of the "Beagle Brigade" first started in 2001 at the NDDTC when then-instructor Susan Ellis trained four handler-and-dog teams to pass the CGC Test. For a while, the CGC Program was optional training for detector dogs in addition to the basic classroom and scent-detection work. After a while, Ellis reported that she noticed an increase in the handler-dog bonding in teams that had CGC training, saying, "I felt the CGC created far more focused and confident teams."

Boy Scouts

Founded in 1910, the Boy Scouts of America (now known as Scouts BSA) recognizes scouts who have earned awards and merit badges related to many practical skills. Canine Good Citizen was added to the "Dog Care" merit badge curriculum, showing that the Scouts truly recognize the merit of the CGC Program.

4-H

The first 4-H clubs began in the early 1900s to benefit rural youth. When many people now hear "4-H," they think of a young person showing a cow or goat at the county fair. While agriculture continues to be an important part of 4-H, this a modern organization that has kept up with the times and is no longer focused primarily on farm-related training. Currently, more than 6.5 million children aged five to nineteen are members of 4-H. These young people are working on projects related to the four Hs—head,

In 4-H programs across the country, children work to earn the Canine Good Citizen award with their dogs.

heart, hands, and health. With the US Department of Agriculture as its parent organization, 4-H has maintained as its slogan: "Learn by Doing."

The training that 4-H offers addresses practical skills in the areas of citizenship, leadership, healthy living, science, and technology. And don't forget the dogs! More than 150,000 young people in 4-H clubs across the country are busy learning about dog training, dog care, 4-H dog shows, Rally, obedience, and agility. The AKC's Canine Good Citizen Test has been added to the 4-H Leader Guide as a starting point for beginning dog trainers.

Community Colleges

In a number of cities, the Canine Good Citizen Program has graduated and gone to college. In 2002, Mary Leatherberry, a CGC Evaluator in New Mexico, started a model CGC Program at Santa Fe Community College. Dog training classes became some of the most popular continuing-education offerings, and the CGC Test Items provided the framework for the class.

Since then, a number of community colleges have added Canine Good Citizen training to the curriculum. Canine Good Citizen classes are available at Rogue Community College in Grants Pass, Oregon, and Dallas County Community College in Dallas, Texas. At Gordon State College in Barnesville, Georgia, Mary Leslie Wilson taught CGC classes. Graduates went on to train in Rally, obedience, and agility. When Wilson asked students about their goals for training their dogs, most indicated that they wanted well-behaved pets and that CGC training was the way to meet this objective.

The rising interest in dog training classes has also been noticed at Columbia-Greene Community College in Hudson, New York. "Dogs are trending, so to speak," said Robert Bodratti, the college's director of community services. Seeing the demand for dog training classes on the increase, Columbia-Greene provided courses taught by AKC CGC Evaluator Edith Rodegerdts.

Housing

It can be difficult to find an apartment to rent or a condo to purchase in a multi-unit building if you own a dog. Fortunately, more and more property managers are realizing that the bond between people and their pets is important. The AKC's Canine Good Citizen Program has been used as a part of the pet policies in an increasing number of housing situations.

In some cases, the management meets with owners, and all owners simply sign the CGC Responsible Dog Owner's Pledge. In other cases, dogs are required to undergo training and actually pass the CGC Test. That's the case at the Tanner Place Condominiums in Portland, Oregon. Developed by Hoyt Street Properties, Tanner Place is part of the revitalization of Portland's Pearl District neighborhood. The upscale condo complex includes studios, one- and two-bedroom units, and penthouses. Owners can have dogs at Tanner Place, but they need to show proof that their dogs have passed the Canine Good Citizen Test.

An incentive-based program is in place for the residents of the Eagle Landing Apartments in Bend, Oregon. Committed to having resident dogs that are well-behaved, the progressive apartment managers of Eagle Landing offer a bonus of one month's free rent for owners of dogs who have earned the Canine Good Citizen certificate.

In housing situations, the Canine Good Citizen program (particularly the Responsible Dog Owner's Pledge) helps property managers and owners say, "We know you love your dogs. You can have them here, but these are the conditions."

Boarding Kennels

Kennels used to be places where you dropped off your dog when you went on vacation. The dog was given a run to stay in along with food and water, and that was the extent of the services. Not anymore. Nowadays, an increasing number of kennels are high-end facilities that can meet all of your dog's needs.

Rio Gran Dog Boarding in Hastings, Minnesota, is one such state-of-the-art facility. Rio Gran is a 15,000-square-foot (close to 1,400-sq-m) pet resort that includes fifty

Rio Gran Kennels in Hastings, Minnesota, is an exemplar of modern-day kennels that offer a full range of services—including Canine Good Citizen training and testing.

themed luxury suites. The building interior has a city theme, making the hallway of suites appear like something straight out of a Disney hotel for humans.

The owners of Rio Gran are on to something! They understand two things about today's dog owners: (1) they love their dogs and (2) they want to have fun with their dogs. To that end, Rio Gran also has a training academy where dog owners can bring their dogs for lessons, or the dogs can attend classes while being boarded. Classes offered include obedience, trick training, flyball, Rally, disc dog, and, of course, preparation and training for the Canine Good Citizen Test.

Rio Gran owner Karen Beskau said about CGC's role at Rio Gran, "We're here to help owners enjoy their dogs and feel good about when the dogs stay with us. Our ongoing CGC classes and CGC testing provide an excellent first step in training. The CGC title is something owners and dogs can achieve together. When dogs have basic training and good manners, we find that our job is much easier when it comes time to board the dogs."

Legislation

In 1990, Florida dog fanciers were working hard to pass a statewide dangerous-dog law that would protect citizens and meet animal-control needs while at the same time not penalizing responsible dog owners. During many of the committee meetings, legislators would say things to the effect of, "We can pass restrictive legislation, but what kind of programs can we implement that are positive, proactive, and designed to educate the public about dogs?" The answer every time? The AKC's Canine Good Citizen Program.

The following year, in 1991, the Florida legislature passed the country's first Canine Good Citizen resolution. If you think back to your high-school civics days, you might remember that a resolution is not a law; it is simply an endorsement or acknowledgment. A law has enforcement power, so if you break a law, you can be punished with a fine or jail time. While legislative resolutions (some states have passed CGC proclamations rather than resolutions) have no enforcement power, they are an excellent vehicle for educating legislators about what the CGC Program is, what responsible dog ownership means, and the benefits of training.

As of 2019, forty-eight states and the United States Senate had passed Canine Good Citizen resolutions, acknowledging that problems related to dogs are really problems related to owners who need to be more responsible, and that training for dogs and people is the solution.

Pet Licensing

In many cities, pet-licensing programs are used to partially fund animal-control services. Years ago, as a result of the work of local AKC clubs and AKC Field

Representative Bill Holbrook, the city of Sequim (in Clallam County, Washington) was the first city to offer licensing discounts when dogs passed the Canine Good Citizen test. Currently, Clallam County offers a 10 percent discount on licenses to owners of dogs that have earned the CGC award.

In July 2009, the Board of County Commissioners in Clackamas County, Oregon, authorized Dog Services to implement a new dog-licensing incentive program. Owners of dogs that have passed the CGC Test are eligible for a 25 percent dog-licensing discount annually for the lifetimes of those dogs. Diana Hallmark, Manager of Clackamas County Dog Services, reported, "The initial response to the CGC incentive program has been very positive. Dog Services has been receiving requests about CGC and dog training from both community dog owners and our community veterinarians. Our hope is that more owners will spend quality time with their canine companions and provide the training necessary to ensure their dogs are excellent neighbors, which in turn will reduce the number of complaints and service requests to which Clackamas County Dog Officers must respond."

Military

Families who live on military bases often have pets. Canine Good Citizen testing has been encouraged and supported by military veterinarians (with assistance from local CGC Evaluators and dog trainers) at a number of military bases, including Fort Bragg (North Carolina), Fort Rucker (Alabama), and Fort Polk (Louisiana).

The Dunes Dog Training Club hosted a CGC training class especially for veterans and their canine companions.

Trainer and CGC Evaluator Joel Norton directs a dog and owner at Hollywood Paws, a Los Angeles-based program that prepares animals for film work. At Hollywood Paws, the CGC Test is administered regularly.

Movies

"Quiet on the set! And … action!" Everyone on the set of movies and Broadway productions needs to follow the director's instructions, and that includes the canine actors. Housed on the campus of the Los Angeles Center Studios, Hollywood Paws prepares animals for professional studio work in movies, television, and commercials. Hollywood Paws trainers work with owners and their dogs from basic obedience to advanced on-film performances. Hollywood Paws recognizes the importance of good manners for canine movie stars and beloved pets alike, and they administer the Canine Good Citizen Test on a regular basis.

Hollywood Paws has a variety of dogs (and cats) that are either ready to do production work (including movies and television) or in training. If a pet owner has a dream of making his dog a star, Hollywood Paws is the place to go. Training focuses on overcoming the challenges unique to movie sets and working in front of a camera.

On a movie set, dogs must go from CGC-level distractions to more difficult distractions, such as lying down and playing dead while food service walks by with lunch and an actress is shrieking and crying. Additionally, the dog's ability to work at a distance from the handler and perform complex chains of behavior (e.g., sit, then move back 20 feet (6m) and quickly lie down) are critical. In CGC training, dogs learn to follow their owners' verbal cues. In Hollywood, this skill develops into an advanced behavior called a "work away," meaning that the dog must work with his owner out of sight and listen for the owner's verbal cues.

There are three levels of classes at Hollywood Paws, and dogs take the CGC Test at the end of the first level. Graduation from Level Two means that dogs are eligible to be considered for production jobs.

Joel Norton, the head trainer and production coordinator at Hollywood Paws, explains why they've adopted the Canine Good Citizen Test. "The CGC is important to us because it allows a third party to check the progress of our dogs in terms of basic obedience," says Norton. "Since the CGC Test revolves around control of one's dog, it is a perfect fit for a graduation test for our Level One program. CGC testing is not a requirement for movie dogs from the standard animal-rental companies, but because we use dogs belonging to private citizens, CGC testing provides peace of mind that everyone appreciates."

So, who are some of the canine movies stars who have earned the Canine Good Citizen award? Perhaps Norton's most recognizable actor is the Golden Retriever named Scout from the movie *Air Buddies.* Step aside Brad Pitt, Scout has also appeared in an Orkin commercial, in blood-pressure medication ads, and in the CBS show *NUMB3RS.* Other Hollywood Paws graduates include dogs that have performed in television pilots and movies, in shows on MTV and E!, and televised ads for major corporations such as Verizon, Microsoft, Burger King, and Nickelodeon.

Parks
Dog Parks

Dog parks are fenced areas where owners can allow their dogs to run off leash. Some dog parks are fenced areas within larger town parks, some are attached to residential areas in large metropolitan areas, and some are privately owned parks for which dog owners can purchase memberships. Dog parks range from simple fenced-in grassy areas with no amenities to areas that resemble canine country clubs.

Misty Pines Dog Park in Sewickley, Pennsylvania, is an outstanding dog park. Dogs can enjoy the fenced playgrounds, hiking trails, agility courses, and water activities, including swimming and dock diving. Misty Pines has separate areas for small dogs and puppies.

The AKC's Canine Good Citizen Test is a goal for many dog owners who are members at Misty Pines. An AKC CGC Evaluator who conducts CGC Tests at the dog park said, "For everyone to fully enjoy a dog park, both dogs and their people need to have good manners. The CGC Program provides a really great format for talking about what it means to be responsible and for teaching dogs the basic skills they need to be around other people and dogs." For more information on Misty Pines, see *www. mistypinespetcompany.com.*

City and County Parks

In most places, with the exception of fenced-in dog parks or designated off-leash areas, leash laws require all dogs in public parks to be on leashes. Irresponsible owners sometimes choose to violate leash laws. Their untrained dogs run like maniacs up to other people (and their leashed dogs) while the owners follow behind, yelling, "It's OK, he's friendly!" (We described the "It's OK, he's friendly!" phenomenon in an earlier chapter.)

The American Kennel Club believes that dog owners should adhere to leash laws. However, there are some cases in which it would be helpful to have a dog lawfully off leash in a public park, such as when the dog is involved in an organized sport (e.g., agility demonstration) or training activity. With the help of dog fanciers, dog trainers, and a supportive city staff, Willard Bailey made a difference in Phoenix, Arizona, which established a model that can be used for parks and recreation departments in other cities.

In Phoenix parks, it used to be that if a person practicing for an obedience trial was working with his or her dog off leash, that person was violating the law. After many months; an uncountable number of strategy sessions, presentations, and commission meetings; and a lot of hard work, Bailey and other Phoenix dog trainers were successful in having the Phoenix Leash Law revised so that trainers could work with their dogs off leash. The Canine Good Citizen Program plays a part in the updated Leash Law, known as Phoenix City Code 8-14. The ordinance now says (summarized):

Dog owners must keep their dogs on a leash when the dog is not on the owner's property. Exceptions are made for:

- Working animals used by or at the direction of law enforcement agencies.
- The dog is being exhibited or trained at a kennel club event or official city event.
- The dog is in an approved off-leash area (a dog park).

The owner/custodian is educating and instructing a dog for any nationally recognized dog sport while meeting all of the following conditions:

a. The owner/custodian has a leash in his/her possession,

b. has no other dogs off leash,

c. has the dog within sight and voice range and actively uses sufficient auditory or visual commands to ensure the dog is not harassing or disturbing people or other animals and is not displaying aggression, and

d. must be able to demonstrate upon request of an enforcement officer that the dog will promptly return by direct route upon voice command. The dog must also stay by the owner/custodian after returning.

e. The owner/custodian must have in his/her possession a "dog sport performance title certificate" (e.g., obedience, agility, etc., title) from a nationally recognized dog sport organization or a "Canine Good Citizen" Program certificate from the American Kennel Club.

Rather than break the law, dog owners can work effectively with city and county officials to change ordinances so that they will permit organized dog-training activities in public parks. It's not easy to change a law or have an ordinance revised. It's a long, hard road that requires a systematic approach and the help of many people. But it can be done—just ask the dog trainers in Phoenix who worked effectively to change the system.

Police K9

Police K9 dogs assist police officers with many tasks, ranging from protection and bite work to bomb and narcotics detection. Because dogs working as police K9s so frequently come in contact with the public, police officers know that in addition to their advanced, highly specialized training, these dogs need to be well mannered and safe in the presence of citizens and other animals. For this reason, a number of police K9 dogs have been trained and tested for the CGC award.

Jim Faggiano is an AKC Approved CGC Evaluator. He is also a dog trainer who specializes in police dogs and a POST (Police Officer Standards for Training) Evaluator for the state of California. In addition to testing dogs on K9 police-dog skills, Faggiano administers the AKC's Canine Good Citizen Test during POST evaluations because he believes that a standard recognized by the community is important.

This group of CGC grads includes a service dog in training and a future police dog.

Prison Programs

There are more than 100 prison programs in which inmates (men and women) train dogs. Some inmates are puppy-raisers for service-dog programs, and others train shelter dogs that will be returned to the shelter after training so they can be adopted. The Canine Good Citizen Program is used as the training standard for a number of prison-based dog-training programs.

There is perhaps no better example of a win-win situation than when inmates train shelter dogs for adoption. Inmates get a chance to give back to society, and dogs get the chance to go to new, loving homes.

Shelters/Humane Organizations

Sadly, one of the most common reasons that dogs are relinquished to shelters is that they have behavior problems. Many of these problems could be easily corrected with basic training (of both the dog and the owner). To help dogs get a good start toward successful placements in adoptive homes, many shelters now have Canine Good Citizen training programs for their dogs. For shelters that don't have paid trainers or behaviorists, volunteers from local dog clubs or the community provide training. Some shelters allow the shelter staff to attend dog-training sessions and get involved in training. This is an uplifting and wonderful experience for the staff, who spend a lot of their time dealing with problems and difficult issues.

Shelter-based CGC programs use the CGC-Ready model to train and prepare dogs for the CGC test. Dogs go through the test with their new owners when they are adopted.

Rescue Groups

Rescue groups are groups that remove dogs from shelters or problem situations (e.g., the owner died and the dog is left homeless). One of the primary functions of rescue groups is to place dogs in loving homes. In addition to providing medical care for dogs that need it, many rescue groups are beginning to provide training to dogs that were given up because of

After living in an abusive situation, Phoenix was rehabilitated with care and training, earning her CGC title.

behavior problems. These dogs usually stay in foster homes, where they are trained by their volunteer foster families before adoption. An increasing number of rescue groups are using the CGC-Ready Program to prepare dogs to take the CGC test with their adoptive owners.

The Welsh Springer Spaniel Club of America (WSSCA) is just one of many exemplars when it comes to the incredible rescue work done across the country by devoted members of AKC national parent clubs. An example of the WSSCA's rescue results follows.

A responsible Welsh Springer Spaniel owner stipulated that her dogs would go to her family when she died. The owner died, the family took the dogs, and, within a short period of time, they decided that they could not keep the dogs. WSSCA rescue was contacted. A WSSCA rescue committee member in Kansas worked with the family to get the dogs, and she cared for them until another member could assist with their placements. A second WSSCA rescue committee member took time off from work, drove from West Virginia to Kansas, and took five dogs with her back to West Virginia. After grooming the dogs and taking them for complete veterinary checkups, the WSSCA carefully screened potential adopters and eventually placed all five dogs in loving homes.

This dedicated AKC national parent club and many others like it across the country work tirelessly to ensure that the breeds they love do not end up in shelters. The American Kennel Club currently registers nearly 200 breeds. Each of those breeds has a national parent club, and we are extremely proud that most have organized, active rescue groups. Volunteers are always needed to foster dogs, help with transportation to new homes, and serve as breed resources for local shelters. To get involved in rescue

Therapy dog Massimo is a favorite guest at a library's reading program.

with a breed you love, go to www.akc.org, click on "Breeds," go to the breed that interests you, and click on "Find Rescues."

Therapy Dogs

Each year, tens of thousands of therapy dogs and their owners visit hospitals, nursing homes, schools, developmental-disabilities programs, and numerous other settings to make people happy and, in some cases, teach new skills. Many therapy dog programs require CGC testing as a prerequisite for participation in their programs. It's important to note that therapy dogs are *not* service dogs, and they do not have the same public-access privileges as service dogs.

Service Dogs

Service dogs are dogs that assist people with disabilities. Each service dog is trained to perform specific tasks related to his person's disability. Earning the Canine Good Citizen award does not give your dog the same special-access rights to public places (restaurants, planes, stores, etc.) that service dogs have. People with disabilities have struggled for decades for the right to have their canine helpers with them in public places, and it would be absolutely unethical to use the CGC award for the purpose of alleging that a dog is a service animal.

Having said this, there are a number of people with disabilities who want their service dogs to pass the Canine Good Citizen Test. Even though these dogs have very advanced skills, such as opening refrigerator doors, holding and giving a check to a bank teller, and picking up a dropped cell phone, many service-dog owners want their dogs to pass the test of good manners best known to the general public—the AKC's Canine Good Citizen Test.

Search and Rescue

Because of their amazing hearing, ability to see well at night, extraordinary sense of smell, and physical endurance, dogs are the tools of choice when it comes to locating missing persons. Good search and rescue (SAR) dogs not only need the ability to find a missing person, they also need the good manners and training that is required to behave appropriately when the person is found. A SAR dog that is aggressive toward people or other animals would not be of much use in a search situation in which many people and dogs are involved.

In 1997, the National Association for Search and Rescue (NASAR) outlined a standardized curriculum for the NASAR SAR Dog Certification Program. The Canine Good Citizen Test is one of the accepted behavioral assessments for dogs according to the NASAR requirements.

If you are interested in search and rescue, know that this work is serious business, and the dog's work is only part of the equation. The life of a person who is injured can depend on what you, the human, do when your dog finds the person. SAR certification requires a great deal of training for the handler. Handlers must pass first-aid courses or have medical training, complete incident-management training, receive training and certification on specific rescue techniques, and be certified in cardiac pulmonary resuscitation (CPR). It is a big commitment for both handler and dog.

Veterinarians

The veterinarian is often the first animal-care professional that dog owners will come to know and trust. In recent years, CGC Programs have been implemented in a variety of veterinary settings.

In 1997, Michael A. Lappin, DVM implemented a model Canine Good Citizen Program in his Massachusetts veterinary clinic. Featured in an article in the *AKC Gazette*, this program served as the inspiration for many other veterinary clinics around the country. The key features of Dr. Lappin's CGC program were:

- Information given to all clients regarding the benefits of CGC.
- CGC training to clients and non-clients during non-clinic hours.
- CGC testing following training sessions.
- A 10 percent discount on services to dogs that earned the CGC award or more advanced obedience titles.
- A CGC mention on the recall cards sent to clients (e.g., "Just a reminder that it is time for Buddy's annual exam and vaccines. Remember, if your dog passes the CGC test, you can receive a discount on veterinary services. Contact us for information on Canine Good Citizen training and testing.").

Dr. Lappin understood that training a dog enhances the bond between the dog and the owner. For veterinarians, there are other bonuses to well-trained dogs. An article in *Veterinary Economics* magazine pointed out the financial benefits of well-behaved pets in veterinary clinics. When a veterinarian can handle a dog without one or more assistants, those staff members can be working on other tasks. More gets done during the day, resulting in additional revenue. When a veterinarian has to spend thirty minutes getting a dog under control so he or she can examine the dog, the dog is agitated, the owner is humiliated, the vet may be frustrated or even at risk of getting bitten, so you can see how trying to manage an untrained dog can turn into an ordeal.

Dr. Michael A. Lappin is a pioneer in introducing CGC principles into his veterinary practice.

The Canine Good Citizen Program has also had a role in university training programs for veterinarians. Dr. M. Josephine Deubler was one of the great women of the dog world. The first female graduate of the University of Pennsylvania School of Veterinary Medicine, Dr. Deubler received her VMD in 1938 and was a member of the faculty of the veterinary school for more than fifty years. The genetic-disease testing laboratory at the University of Pennsylvania bears her name.

With decades of experience as an exhibitor, dog-show judge, and leader in the field of animal welfare, Dr. Deubler recognized the potential benefits of the Canine Good Citizen Program for dogs and their owners. She understood that many dog owners would talk to their veterinarians about behavioral issues and that proactive early training is crucial.

When she heard about the Canine Good Citizen Program during a dinner conversation at a dog show, Dr. Deubler went into action. Within several weeks, the University of Pennsylvania School of Veterinary Medicine had received CGC materials, and the veterinary students and dog owners effectively used the CGC Program to learn from each other.

At the University of Florida, Cynda Crawford DVM, PhD is best known as the nationally recognized researcher who made a major discovery related to the canine influenza virus. While most days in the lab focus on science, Dr. Crawford has also been the faculty advisor to veterinary students who administer the Canine Good Citizen Test and evaluate dogs for therapy work. These young vets go into the world as well-respected professionals who are equipped to help dog owners understand that canine health is both physical and behavioral.

Work Settings

The therapeutic benefits of dogs are well documented. For those of us who love them, science tells us that dogs can lower our blood pressure and reduce stress. And perhaps nowhere do we need stress relief more than when we are at work.

The American Kennel Club's Raleigh, North Carolina, office has a Dogs-in-the-Building Program that has been used as a model for other programs around the country. Dogs that come to work with AKC employees must:

- Pass the Canine Good Citizen and AKC Community Canine tests. The owner has to sign the Responsible Dog Owner's Pledge as a part of CGC testing.
- Have a veterinarian certify that the dog is in good health.
- Have proof of rabies vaccines.
- Have a flea/tick-prevention program in place.
- Demonstrate skills that are beyond CGC, such as the ability to stay in an office, be quiet, and not cause trouble during the day. Owners put baby gates across their doorways and use crates when appropriate.

Dogs aren't the only ones who need to follow the rules at work. Owners agree to:

- Walk dogs only in designated areas.
- Clean up after their dogs.
- Identify a "backup" human buddy for the dog who can take the dog out if necessary, help if there is a problem and the owner is in a meeting, etc. A sign (with a picture of the dog, the owner's and dog's names, and the designated buddy) is posted by the office door.
- Use only the designated "dog elevators." This accommodates people with allergies and building occupants who may be afraid of dogs.
- Respect the rights of nearby staff members who may have allergies to animals. In such a case, the health of the worker with the allergy comes first.
- Respect the rights of visitors and building "neighbors" (the Raleigh building is shared by other companies) by recognizing that some people are afraid of dogs and/or do not wish to interact with dogs.
- Not allow the dog to interfere with productivity and work progress.
- Provide documentation of homeowner's insurance or renter's insurance (for liability).
- Follow any recommendations of the Dogs-in-the-Building committee when there is a problem.

HOW THE AKC HELPS
EVERY DOG OWNER

Here at the American Kennel Club, we're far more than dog shows. We say that we're not just champion dogs—we're the dogs' champion. This chapter outlines some of our many services and programs that haven't been covered in earlier chapters.

Founded in 1884, the AKC has more than 5,000 dog clubs and more than 22,000 events of varying types each year. The AKC is a "club made up of clubs." This means that, as an individual, you can't become a member of the AKC. The members are dog clubs from all over the country, and it is these clubs that serve as the guardians for individual breeds.

The AKC encourages owners to take their dogs' training to the next level and enjoy the competitive opportunities that local AKC clubs provide.

AKC Museum of the Dog

Holding one of the largest collections of dog-related fine art in the world, the AKC Museum of the Dog celebrates the role of dogs in society. Fine art is combined with high-tech interpretive displays to make this award-winning museum one of the finest anywhere. Formerly located in St. Louis, the museum's home is now 101 Park Avenue in New York City.

AKC Reunite

We all love our dogs and take every precaution to protect them, but sometimes accidents happen, and a dog gets lost. AKC Reunite (formerly Companion Animal Recovery) provides lifetime recovery services for pets who have a microchip, tattoo, or collar tag bearing their contact information. AKC Reunite is on the job, ready to help lost pets get home 24 hours a day, 365 days a year. Since 1995, more than 500,000 lost pets have been successfully reunited with their families.

Canine Health Foundation

The mission statement of the AKC Canine Health Foundation (CHF) is to "develop resources for basic and applied health programs with an emphasis on canine genetics to improve the overall quality of life for dogs and their owners." CHF works diligently to eliminate genetic disorders in dogs. The research done by CHF benefits all dogs, purebred and mixed breed alike.

Clubs/Club Relations

The AKC has clubs across the country, including specialty clubs (clubs for one specific breed), all-breed clubs for conformation, performance clubs, obedience clubs (clubs that teach obedience, Rally, and sometimes agility), agility clubs, and more. If you are interested in training your dog, check out an AKC club near you. You'll find experienced trainers who can help you achieve your training and competition objectives. You'll have the chance to meet and train with a wonderful group of people who share your love of dogs. To find the AKC club near you, go to www.akc.org and click on "Clubs."

Customer Relations

When you have a question and need help, the friendly staff in the AKC's Customer Service Call Center will assist you. The customer service department handles nearly 55,000 questions per month and hundreds of emails per day that range from registration issues to ordering Canine Good Citizen Test kits. Customer service hours are weekdays between 8:30 a.m. and 5:00 p.m. (ET).

DNA

The AKC's DNA Operations Department uses the most modern DNA technology to help dogs. This department uses DNA technology to establish the genetic identity of dogs. Collecting a DNA sample is a painless process that involves using a small brush to swab the inside of the dog's cheek. Loose cells stick to the swab and are a source of DNA that can be analyzed.

Handlers Program

Dogs can be shown in conformation dog shows by their owners, friends, or professional handlers. The AKC Registered Handlers Program was started in order to ensure that the health and welfare of all dogs in the care of handlers is maintained. To participate in this program, handlers must complete an application process, meet certain criteria, and adhere to a Code of Ethics.

Judges' Education

The education of judges is obviously important for conformation dog shows, but the judges' role goes beyond the show ring. AKC judges receive intensive hands-on training at seminars and institutes around the country. They become experts on individual breeds—the movement, physical structure, any health problems the breed might have, temperament, and so on. Having a cadre of well-trained experts can be beneficial to anyone who is considering a purebred dog.

Legislation

What was once the AKC Canine Legislation Department is now called AKC Government Relations. This is the department that monitors dog-related legislation and serves as a resource to dog fanciers who are addressing legislative issues.

Library

If you love dogs, you should visit the American Kennel Club's library at least once. Housed at the AKC's New York City office at 101 Park Avenue, the library has more than 19,000 volumes, including 2,500 rare books, magazines, stamps, bookplates, and videos. Because the library has one of the most impressive dog-book collections in the world, there's a good chance you'll see writers and scholars who are working on their latest manuscripts.

Publications

If you want to learn more about dogs, the AKC has several publications that may interest you. *The AKC Gazette* is a digital monthly all-breed magazine that includes articles covering all aspects of dogs. *AKC Family Dog* is a bi-monthly magazine that includes practical articles written in an entertaining style for today's busy dog owner.

There are many ways that a CGC dog can become involved in his community.

Public Education

The AKC's Public Education Division works to educate the humans in a dog's life. The goal of AKC Public Education is to teach responsible dog ownership and the joys of participating in dog activities to dog owners, the general public, educators, and legislators. Volunteers from AKC clubs serve as Canine Ambassadors who visit schools and other youth programs to teach about topics such as safety around dogs and responsible ownership.

Website

If you haven't yet visited the AKC's website, take a moment and go to *www.akc.org*. If you are interested in dogs, you're in for a treat when you visit the website that has been described as the most popular dog-related address on the Internet. You can read the latest news pertaining to dog-related issues, shop at the online store, learn about breeds, find breed rescue groups, locate upcoming events to participate in or attend as a spectator, find a trainer or Evaluator for CGC or AKC S.T.A.R. Puppy—and much more!

INDEX

work settings, 181
Sprung, Dennis, 7
S.T.A.R. Puppy training, AKC, 58, 122, 133, 147–148
stationary visual distractions, 110
stay command, teaching, 75–78
stimulus control, 27, 71
strangers. *See Accepting a Friendly Stranger test*
staying home alone, 125
Supervised Separation test
    barking during, 118
    boredom, preventing, 122–123
    comfort, 125
    crate training, 132
    description of, 114–117
    destructive behavior, 117–119
    exercise, 123
    familiar sounds, 123–124
    multiple-pet interactions, 124
    schedules, 123
    separation behaviors, 119–120
    shaping behaviors, 121
    unsupervised separation at home, 117–119,
      121–124
systematic training, 121

T

tactile stimulation (touch), 51
tattoos, 136
teeth, care of, 51
Temperament Test, AKC (ATT), 28, 104, 155
therapy dogs, 9, 66–67, 152, 177
thunder, desensitization to, 109–110
toy breeds, 18–19, 133
toys
    to prevent boredom, 122–123
    in training, 55–56
tracking, 159–160
training and testing
    benefits of, 140–141
    Evaluators, meeting, 142
    instructors, choosing, 143–145
    locations for, 143
    retesting, 145

20-foot line, 79

U

underweight dogs, 40
unsupervised separation, 117–119, 121–124
unusual crowds, 66
Urban CGC Test, 63
urinating, inappropriate, 64, 117, 119
US Department of Agriculture, 164, 166, 167

V

variable schedule of reinforcement, 88
verbal cues, 58–59, 76
veterinarians, 131–132, 179–180
Veterinary Economics (magazine), 179
visual distractions, stationary, 110

W

walking your dog, 58–59, 96–97
Walking on a Loose Leash test
    heel position, 56–57
    left-side position, 52
    loose leash, defined, 56
    lure, using food or toy as, 55–56
    starting position, 54–55
    walking, 52–54, 58–59
Walking through a Crowd test
    description of, 60–62
    hiding behind the handler, 67
    manners during, 61–62
    problems related to, 62–64
    teaching, 64–66
    therapy dogs, skills for, 66–67
    unusual crowds, 66
waste, picking up after your dog, 138
water requirements, 132
website, AKC, 185
weight, 40
Welsh Springer Spaniel Club of America
  (WSSCA), 176
Wilson, Mary Leslie, 167
"work away" training, 172
work settings, dog in, 181

Photo Credits

Photos courtesy of:

American Kennel Club *CGC Evaluator News*: 9, 14, 16, 33, 39, 53, 67, 70, 103, 107, 110, 122, 127, 128, 138, 142, 144, 148, 149, 151–154, 158, 164–168, 170, 171, 174, 175, 177, 182, 185

Sherry Berliner: 6, 146

Mary Bloom: 25, 65, 76, 118, 147, 178

Mary Burch: 8, 28, 91, 94, 116, 148, 155

Cynda Crawford: 36

Marti Hohmann: 13, 59

iStock by Getty Images: PeopleImages: 23; Ksenia Raykova: 35; SolStock: 20

Tamra Krystinik: 1

Michael A. Lappin: 180

James Leatherberry: 26, 37, 42, 51, 79, 83, 96, 97, 101, 105, 111

Tanya Lee: 154 (bottom)

Ralph Orlando: 63, 150

Shutterstock: Coffeemill: 160; cunaplus: 121; cynoclub: 45; Droidworker (sidebar background): 8, 15, 23, 30, 62, 72, 75, 81, 98, 102, 113, 117, 119, 134, 139, 143, 159; Fotyma: 52; Brian Goodman: 163; Eric Isselee: 34, 123, 137; Jagodka: 176; Saravut Khusrisuwan: 81; l i g h t p o e t: 84; mikumistock: 49; Photofollies: 48; ANURAK PONGPATIMET: 15; Skumer: 157; takayuki: 140; textu: 183

David Woo: 5, 7, 11, 12, 18, 19, 21, 22, 27, 31, 40, 41, 43, 46, 47, 54, 55, 57, 58, 61, 69, 72–75, 77, 78, 80, 85–87, 89, 93, 95, 100, 106, 115, 120, 125, 133, 135, 141